AF414741

Table of Contents

Somalia: A Painful History of Struggle and Resistance

Copyright Page

Title: Somalia: A Painful History of Struggle and Resistance

1ST Edition

ISBN: 978-1-312-11386-2

Somalia: A Painful History of Struggle and Resistance

By Roberto Miguel Rodriguez

Chapter 1: Somalia: History of a Country in Pain

Precolonial Somalia: Cultural and Historical Background

Introduction:

In order to understand the present-day struggles and resilience of Somalia, it is essential to delve into its rich and diverse precolonial history. This subchapter aims to provide diplomats, educators, teachers, journalists, politicians, and legislators with a comprehensive overview of the cultural and historical background of Somalia before the era of colonialism.

1. Geography and Trade:

Situated in the Horn of Africa, Somalia boasts a strategic location along major trade routes. Its coastline, stretching over 3,300 kilometers, has historically facilitated trade with neighboring regions, including the Arabian Peninsula, Persia, India, and East Africa. The exchange of goods, ideas, and cultures played a crucial role in shaping the Somali society.

2. Ancient Civilizations:

Somalia was home to several ancient civilizations, such as the Land of Punt, which existed as early as 2500 BCE. The Land of Punt served as a vital hub for trade with ancient Egypt, providing valuable resources like frankincense, myrrh, and exotic animals.

3. Somali Clans:

Clan dynamics have long been an integral part of Somali society. Clans, known as "qabiil," have played a significant role in governance, social organization, and dispute resolution. Understanding the influence of clans is crucial to comprehending the political landscape of precolonial Somalia.

4. Islamic Influence:

Somalia embraced Islam in the 7th century, which profoundly influenced its culture, society, and governance. Islam became a unifying force, fostering a shared religious identity and providing a framework for social order.

5. Art and Literature:

Precolonial Somalia witnessed a flourishing of art and literature. Oral tradition played a vital role in preserving history, passing down folktales, and celebrating poetry and music. Prominent Somali scholars emerged, contributing to the intellectual and cultural development of the region.

6. Kingdoms and Sultanates:

Several powerful kingdoms and sultanates emerged in precolonial Somalia, including the Sultanate of Adal, the Ajuran Empire, and the Geledi Sultanate. These entities exerted political and economic influence, engaging in trade, diplomacy, and warfare with neighboring powers.

Conclusion:

The precolonial era of Somalia provides a glimpse into the rich cultural heritage and historical complexity of the region. Understanding the dynamics of trade, ancient civilizations, clan systems, Islamic influence, art and literature, and the rise of kingdoms and sultanates is crucial for comprehending the challenges and opportunities faced by modern-day Somalia. By delving into its past, diplomats, educators, teachers, journalists, politicians, and legislators can gain a deeper understanding of the country's history, resilience, and potential for development.

The Ancient Kingdoms of Somalia

Throughout history, Somalia has been home to several ancient kingdoms that have left a lasting impact on its culture and society. Understanding the history of these kingdoms is crucial to comprehending the country's present-day struggles and resilience. This subchapter delves into the ancient kingdoms of Somalia, shedding light on their significance and contribution to the nation's rich heritage.

One of the most prominent ancient kingdoms in Somalia was the Kingdom of Punt. Located in the region known as the Horn of Africa, Punt thrived between 2500 and 1500 BCE. This kingdom was a major trade hub and played a pivotal role in connecting Africa, Asia, and Europe. Its strategic location along the Red Sea allowed it to establish commercial networks that stretched from Egypt to India. The Kingdom of Punt's wealth and influence were driven by its abundant resources, including gold, ivory, and incense.

Another noteworthy ancient kingdom in Somalia was the Kingdom of Aksum. Flourishing between the first and seventh centuries CE, Aksum was renowned for its powerful navy and trade routes. It controlled vast territories in the Red Sea and Indian Ocean, making it a dominant force in the region. The Kingdom of Aksum's adoption of Christianity in the fourth century CE also contributed to its cultural and religious influence.

The Sultanate of Adal was yet another significant ancient kingdom in Somalia. Emerging in the 9th century CE, it was a Muslim state that played a crucial role in spreading Islam in the region. The Sultanate of Adal engaged in fierce conflicts with the Ethiopian Empire and European powers, leaving a profound impact on the political and religious landscape of the Horn of Africa.

The ancient kingdoms of Somalia laid the foundation for the country's cultural diversity and resilience. They fostered trade, promoted knowledge exchange, and established diplomatic relations with neighboring regions. Today, Somalia's ancient history serves as a reminder of its potential for growth, development, and stability.

This subchapter is essential for diplomats, educators, teachers, journalists, politicians, and legislators as it provides historical context to understand Somalia's complex present. Furthermore, it appeals to the niches of Somali history, political instability, cultural identity, gender equality, and economic development. By examining the ancient kingdoms of Somalia, readers gain a deeper understanding of the country's past, which is crucial for shaping its future.

Islam's Arrival and Influence in Somalia

Throughout history, Somalia has been shaped by various cultural, religious, and political influences. One of the most significant and enduring of these is Islam. The arrival of Islam in Somalia dates back to the 7th century, brought by Arab traders and missionaries. Over time, Islam became deeply ingrained in Somali society, playing a central role in shaping its culture, politics, and everyday life.

The spread of Islam in Somalia was not just a religious phenomenon; it was also a catalyst for social, economic, and political change. As Somali merchants embraced Islam, they expanded their trade networks across the Indian Ocean, connecting Somalia to the wider Islamic world. This trade brought wealth and prosperity to the region, fostering the growth of urban centers and contributing to the development of a cosmopolitan Somali society.

The influence of Islam can be seen in various aspects of Somali life. Islamic teachings and principles have influenced the legal system, with Sharia law serving as a basis for the Somali legal framework. Islamic education and scholarship have also played a significant role in the intellectual and educational development of the Somali population.

Furthermore, Islam has had a profound impact on Somali politics. Islamic groups have often played a prominent role in the country's political landscape. The rise of Islamic political movements, such as Al-Ittihad Al-Islamiya and Al-Shabaab, has been a result of complex historical, social, and political dynamics in Somalia. These groups have sought to establish an Islamic state in Somalia, impacting both domestic politics and international relations.

In recent years, efforts have been made to promote a moderate interpretation of Islam in Somalia, aiming to counter the radicalization and violence associated with extremist groups. Islamic scholars, educators, and religious leaders have played a crucial role in promoting a peaceful and inclusive understanding of Islam, emphasizing its values of tolerance, compassion, and social justice.

In conclusion, Islam's arrival and influence in Somalia have been significant factors in shaping the country's history, culture, and politics. As Somalia continues to rebuild and navigate its path towards stability and development, understanding and appreciating the role of Islam in Somali society is essential. By recognizing the diverse interpretations and practices of Islam in Somalia, diplomats, educators, teachers, journalists, politicians, and legislators can contribute to fostering dialogue, understanding, and cooperation in the country, ultimately supporting Somalia's journey towards peace, prosperity, and resilience.

Somali Trade and Commerce in the Precolonial Era

In the subchapter titled "Somali Trade and Commerce in the Precolonial Era," we delve into the rich history of Somalia's vibrant trade and commerce scene before the arrival of colonial powers. This discussion aims to provide diplomats, educators, teachers, journalists, politicians, and legislators with a comprehensive understanding of Somalia's economic prowess and its impact on the country's development.

Somalia, situated at the crossroads of the Red Sea and the Indian Ocean, has long been a hub of international trade. From ancient times, Somali traders established strong commercial networks and traversed vast distances, connecting the African continent with the Arab world, Persia, India, and even as far as China. These trading routes brought prosperity and cultural exchange to the region, shaping a unique Somali identity.

The precolonial Somali economy was primarily based on maritime trade, with bustling ports such as Zeila, Mogadishu, and Berbera serving as significant trading centers. Somali merchants, known as Banadiris, mastered the art of navigation and shipbuilding, enabling them to engage in long-distance trade expeditions. They traded in a wide range of commodities, including valuable spices, gold, ivory, and slaves.

The Somali people also developed a distinct economic system known as the "Xeer," a customary law that governed trade and commerce. This system promoted fair business practices, protected property rights, and resolved disputes through mediation. The Xeer played a crucial role in fostering trust and stability, making Somalia an attractive destination for foreign traders.

Furthermore, Somali society was organized into clans, and each clan had a specific role in commerce. Some clans specialized in livestock herding, while others excelled in agricultural production or trade. This division of labor contributed to a diverse and robust economy, allowing for the exchange of goods and services between different regions of Somalia.

It is important to note that understanding the precolonial era of Somali trade and commerce provides valuable insights into the country's economic potential today. By building upon the historical strengths of maritime trade, Somalia can reestablish itself as a regional economic powerhouse. Efforts to revive and modernize its ports, improve infrastructure, and strengthen trade relations with neighboring countries are key to unlocking Somalia's economic potential.

In conclusion, the subchapter "Somali Trade and Commerce in the Precolonial Era" sheds light on the historical significance of trade and commerce in Somalia. By exploring the country's rich trading history, diplomats, educators, teachers, journalists, politicians, and legislators gain a deeper understanding of the economic challenges and opportunities facing Somalia today. By leveraging the lessons from the past, Somalia can strive towards sustainable economic development and resilience.

Colonial Rule and Its Impact on Somalia

Introduction:

The colonial rule in Somalia, which lasted from the late 19th century until the country gained independence in 1960, had a profound and lasting impact on the nation. This subchapter explores the effects of colonialism on Somalia, focusing on the political, social, and economic consequences that still shape the country today.

Historical Context:

Before delving into the impact of colonial rule, it is essential to understand the historical context in which it occurred. Somalia was divided into five regions, each colonized by a different European power. The British controlled present-day Somaliland and the regions of Jubaland and Northeastern Kenya. The Italians colonized southern Somalia, while the French governed the region of Djibouti. This division laid the foundation for future political and social fragmentation within Somalia.

Political Impact:

Colonial rule significantly altered the political landscape of Somalia. European powers exploited existing clan divisions, playing them against each other for their own benefit. This manipulation created deep-seated clan rivalries that persist to this day. Furthermore, the colonial powers introduced centralized governance systems that weakened traditional Somali governance structures, eroding trust and legitimacy in the eyes of the Somali people.

Social Impact:

The social impact of colonialism in Somalia was equally significant. European powers imposed their cultural values and norms, undermining Somali traditions and heritage. Additionally, the colonial powers introduced a system of education that prioritized European languages and cultures, leading to the marginalization of Somali language and literature. This cultural imposition continues to be a source of tension and struggle for the Somali people.

Economic Impact:

Colonialism also had a profound impact on Somalia's economy. European powers exploited Somalia's resources, primarily its livestock and agricultural products, for their own gain. This extraction of resources created economic dependency and hindered the development of a diversified economy. The legacy of this economic exploitation can still be seen in Somalia's struggle for economic self-sufficiency.

Conclusion:

Colonial rule left an indelible mark on Somalia, shaping its political, social, and economic landscape. The division of the country by European powers, the erosion of traditional governance structures, the imposition of foreign cultural norms, and the economic exploitation all contribute to the challenges faced by Somalia today. Understanding the impact of colonialism is crucial for diplomats, educators, journalists, and politicians seeking to address the complex issues facing Somalia. By acknowledging this painful history, we can work towards a more inclusive and equitable future for the Somali people.

The Scramble for Africa: Somalia's Colonization

In the late 19th century, a wave of European powers embarked on the colonization of Africa, leading to what historians now refer to as the Scramble for Africa. Somalia, situated on the eastern coast of Africa, did not escape the clutches of this colonial onslaught. This subchapter explores the painful period of Somalia's colonization and sheds light on its lasting impact.

The colonization of Somalia can be traced back to the late 19th century when European powers, such as Britain, France, and Italy, began to establish their influence in the region. Britain, with its strategic interests in the Indian Ocean, occupied the northern region of Somalia, known as British Somaliland. Meanwhile, Italy set its sights on the southern part of the country, which eventually became Italian Somaliland.

The colonization of Somalia had far-reaching consequences for the Somali people. The European powers implemented policies that favored their own interests, often at the expense of the local population. The exploitation of resources, forced labor, and oppressive governance became the norm under colonial rule. These practices sowed the seeds of discontent and resistance among the Somali people, setting the stage for future struggles.

Despite the hardships imposed by colonization, the Somali people demonstrated their resilience and determination to regain their independence. The struggle for self-determination gained momentum in the mid-20th century, as nationalist movements emerged across the country. The efforts of Somali leaders, such as Sayid Mohammed Abdullah Hassan and Abdullahi Issa Mohamud, played a crucial role in mobilizing the Somali people and galvanizing the resistance against colonial powers.

Finally, in 1960, Somalia achieved independence and emerged as a sovereign nation. However, the scars of colonization were deep, and the legacy of European rule continued to shape the political, social, and economic dynamics of the country.

Understanding the history of Somalia's colonization is essential for diplomats, educators, teachers, journalists, politicians, and legislators. It provides valuable insights into the challenges faced by the Somali people and the complex dynamics that have shaped the country's trajectory. By studying this chapter, readers will gain a deeper understanding of the historical context that underlies the current issues facing Somalia.

Moreover, this chapter also appeals to specific niches such as Somali civil war, political instability, Somali piracy, Somaliland's struggle for independence, clan dynamics, Somali refugees, Somali women's empowerment, Somali art and literature, and the Somali economy. These topics are interconnected with the history of colonization, as they are all influenced by the legacy of European rule.

Overall, the story of Somalia's colonization is a painful yet crucial part of the country's history. By delving into this subchapter, readers will gain a comprehensive understanding of the impact of colonization on Somalia and its relevance to a range of disciplines and areas of interest.

Italian Somaliland: Assimilation and Resistance

Italian Somaliland, a period of colonization that lasted from the late 19th century to the mid-20th century, left an indelible mark on Somalia and its people. This subchapter delves into the complex relationship between the Italian colonizers and the Somali population, examining both the assimilation efforts imposed by the Italians and the resilient resistance displayed by the Somalis.

Under Italian rule, which began in 1889, the Somalis faced a systematic campaign of assimilation aimed at eradicating their cultural and linguistic heritage. The Italians sought to impose their own language, customs, and governance structures onto the Somali people. Schools were established to teach Italian and promote Italian culture, and the use of the Somali language was discouraged. This assimilation policy aimed to create a sense of Italian identity among the Somalis, erasing their own unique cultural identity.

However, the Somali people fiercely resisted these assimilation efforts. They clung to their language, traditions, and social structures, determined to preserve their distinct heritage. The Somalis organized themselves into clandestine groups, engaging in acts of civil disobedience and rebellion to defy Italian rule. These acts of resistance ranged from cultural expressions such as poetry and songs to armed uprisings against the colonizers.

One notable example of resistance was the Dervish movement led by Sayyid Mohammed Abdullah Hassan. The Dervishes waged a prolonged guerrilla war against the Italians, using their deep knowledge of the Somali terrain to their advantage. Though the Dervishes eventually succumbed to the superior firepower of the Italians, they left an enduring legacy of resistance and defiance among the Somali people.

The Italian assimilation policy and the Somali resistance to it had far-reaching consequences for the Somali nation. While the Italians were eventually driven out of Somalia during World War II, the scars of assimilation and the legacy of resistance continued to shape the Somali identity and the nation's struggles for self-determination.

Understanding the dynamics of assimilation and resistance in Italian Somaliland is crucial for diplomats, educators, journalists, and politicians seeking to comprehend the complexities of Somalia's history and its current challenges. By examining this chapter, readers can gain insights into the resilience of the Somali people and the enduring impact of colonialism on their cultural, social, and political fabric.

As Somalia continues to navigate its path towards stability and development, acknowledging the assimilation and resistance experiences of Italian Somaliland is essential for addressing the challenges faced by the Somali people, promoting inclusivity, and fostering a society built on the principles of self-determination, cultural preservation, and resilience.

British Somaliland: Divide and Rule Policies

In the subchapter titled "British Somaliland: Divide and Rule Policies," we delve into the historical context and consequences of British colonial rule in Somaliland. This chapter aims to provide diplomats, educators, teachers, journalists, politicians, and legislators, as well as individuals interested in the history and politics of Somalia, with a comprehensive understanding of the impact of divide and rule policies implemented by the British.

During the late 19th century, Britain established a colonial presence in the Horn of Africa, including the region known as Somaliland. The British administration employed a strategy of divide and rule, exploiting existing clan rivalries and animosities to maintain control over the region. By favoring certain clans over others and exacerbating inter-clan tensions, the British were able to manipulate the local population and solidify their rule.

One of the most significant consequences of British divide and rule policies was the exacerbation of clan dynamics in Somali society. The colonial administration created a system of indirect rule, appointing clan elders as intermediaries between the British authorities and the local population. This system further entrenched clan-based politics in Somaliland, which continues to shape the political landscape of the country to this day.

Furthermore, the divide and rule policies implemented by the British sowed the seeds of political instability in Somalia. By favoring certain clans and excluding others from positions of power, the colonial administration created deep-seated grievances and a sense of marginalization among those who were left out. This laid the groundwork for future conflicts and power struggles within the country.

The legacy of British divide and rule policies is also evident in the struggle for independence in Somaliland. The marginalization experienced under British rule motivated the people of Somaliland to fight for self-determination. The quest for independence has been a central political struggle in the region, with Somaliland declaring independence from Somalia in 1991. The impact of British divide and rule policies can still be seen today, as the political dynamics between Somaliland and the rest of Somalia remain complex and contentious.

In conclusion, the subchapter on "British Somaliland: Divide and Rule Policies" provides a comprehensive analysis of the historical context and consequences of British colonial rule in Somaliland. It examines how the divide and rule policies employed by the British influenced clan dynamics, contributed to political instability, and shaped the struggle for independence in the region. This chapter serves as an important resource for diplomats, educators, teachers, journalists, politicians, and legislators, as well as individuals interested in the history and politics of Somalia.

Independence and the Formation of the Somali Republic

Introduction:

The subchapter titled "Independence and the Formation of the Somali Republic" delves into the historical background and significance of Somalia gaining independence and establishing itself as a sovereign nation. This chapter explores the struggles faced by the Somali people to attain self-rule and the subsequent formation of the Somali Republic. It aims to provide a comprehensive understanding of the events that shaped the country's history and the impact of independence on various aspects of Somali society, politics, and culture.

Historical Context:

The chapter begins by highlighting the period of colonization, during which Somalia was divided into five regions under the control of different colonial powers. It explores the impact of colonization on Somali society and the subsequent rise of nationalist movements advocating for independence. The chapter emphasizes the role of prominent Somali leaders and their efforts to unite the various regions and secure self-rule.

Struggles for Independence:

This section delves into the challenges faced by the Somali people during their struggle for independence. It discusses the various resistance movements, protests, and negotiations that eventually led to the recognition of Somali sovereignty. The chapter also explores the role of international actors and organizations in supporting Somalia's bid for independence.

Formation of the Somali Republic:

This section focuses on the establishment of the Somali Republic and its early years as an independent nation. It highlights the political structures, institutions, and policies put in place to govern the newly formed republic. The chapter also examines the challenges faced by the young nation and the efforts made to address them.

Impact on Somali Society, Politics, and Culture:

The subchapter concludes by analyzing the impact of independence on various aspects of Somali society. It explores the changes in political dynamics, the growth of democratic institutions, and the challenges faced in nation-building. Additionally, the chapter discusses the revival of Somali culture, literature, and arts as a means of expressing national identity and resilience.

Conclusion:

The subchapter "Independence and the Formation of the Somali Republic" provides a comprehensive account of Somalia's journey to independence and the subsequent establishment of the Somali Republic. It offers valuable insights for diplomats, educators, journalists, and politicians interested in understanding the historical context and significance of Somali independence. The chapter also contributes to the broader themes covered in the book, such as political instability, cultural identity, and economic development, making it a valuable resource for a diverse range of readers.

The Road to Independence: Nationalist Movements

In the subchapter titled "The Road to Independence: Nationalist Movements," we delve into the historical journey of Somalia towards its independence and the role of nationalist movements in shaping the country's destiny. This chapter explores the struggles, sacrifices, and resilience of the Somali people as they fought for self-determination and sovereignty.

The story of Somalia's nationalist movements begins with the European colonization era, during which the Somali territories were divided into five regions: British Somaliland, Italian Somaliland, French Somaliland (Djibouti), Ethiopian Somali Region (Ogaden), and Kenyan Somali territories. However, the Somali people, driven by a shared language, culture, and history, aspired to unite and establish an independent Somali state.

One of the key figures in Somalia's journey to independence was Sayyid Mohammed Abdullah Hassan, also known as the "Mad Mullah." Hassan led a nationalist movement against British and Italian colonial forces in the early 20th century. His resistance, fueled by his religious authority and charismatic leadership, inspired many Somalis to join the fight for independence.

The nationalist movements gained momentum in the mid-20th century, as Somalia's quest for independence became a focal point for the Somali people. Political parties, such as the Somali Youth League (SYL), emerged as prominent advocates for independence. They organized protests, strikes, and demonstrations, demanding an end to colonial rule and the establishment of an independent Somali state.

In 1960, Somalia finally achieved independence, with the union of British Somaliland and Italian Somaliland. This milestone marked the culmination of the nationalist movements' efforts and the beginning of a new era for the Somali people.

The chapter also explores the impact of these nationalist movements on modern-day Somalia. It examines how the struggle for independence shaped the country's political landscape, societal dynamics, and cultural identity. Moreover, it analyzes the challenges and opportunities that arose in the aftermath of independence, providing insight into the complexities of nation-building and statehood.

"The Road to Independence: Nationalist Movements" offers a comprehensive account of Somalia's journey towards self-determination, providing valuable historical context for diplomats, educators, teachers, journalists, politicians, and legislators. Furthermore, it appeals to the niches of "SOMALIA: HISTORY OF A COUNTRY IN PAIN," "Somali Civil War: Causes and Consequences," "Political Instability in Somalia: Origins and Impact," and various other topics related to Somalia's history, politics, society, and culture.

The Challenges of Uniting Somali Territories

Introduction:

The unity of Somali territories has remained a complex and arduous task throughout history. This subchapter aims to shed light on the challenges faced in the pursuit of unifying Somali territories. From historical divisions to political instability, various factors have hindered the establishment of a cohesive Somali state. This chapter is addressed to diplomats, educators, teachers, journalists, politicians, and legislators, as well as those interested in the intricate dynamics of Somali history and politics.

Historical Divisions:

One of the primary challenges of uniting Somali territories can be traced back to historical divisions. The arbitrary borders drawn during the colonial era by European powers divided the Somali people among different territories, such as British Somaliland, Italian Somaliland, French Somaliland, and the Ethiopian Somali Region. These divisions created a fragmented Somali identity, making the task of unification more complex.

Political Instability:

Political instability has plagued Somalia for decades, impeding efforts to unite the territories. The collapse of the central government in 1991 led to a protracted civil war, leaving the country in a state of anarchy. Factionalism, warlordism, and clan-based conflicts have further hindered unity. The lack of a stable government and effective governance structures has made it difficult to establish a strong and unified Somali state.

Clan Dynamics:

Clan dynamics play a significant role in Somali politics and society, posing a challenge to territorial unification. Clans have historically held power and influence, often resulting in political fragmentation and competition. Clan-based conflicts and rivalries have perpetuated divisions and hindered the establishment of a cohesive Somali nation.

International Response:

The international response to the challenges of unifying Somali territories has also posed obstacles. Foreign interventions, conflicting geopolitical interests, and inadequate support for state-building efforts have hindered progress. The lack of a coordinated international approach and the involvement of external actors have often exacerbated existing divisions and prevented the consolidation of Somali territories.

Conclusion:

The challenges of uniting Somali territories are multifaceted and deeply rooted in historical, political, and societal factors. Overcoming these challenges requires a comprehensive understanding of Somalia's complex history and dynamics. It necessitates a concerted effort from both domestic and international actors, focusing on reconciliation, inclusive governance, and nation-building. Only through addressing these challenges can Somalia move towards a unified and resilient nation, capable of overcoming its painful history and embracing a brighter future.

Early Political Developments: Democracy and Dictatorship

Introduction:

In the subchapter titled "Early Political Developments: Democracy and Dictatorship," we explore the historical journey of Somalia's political landscape, highlighting the transition from democratic principles to dictatorial rule. This chapter delves into the key events, actors, and ideologies that shaped Somalia's early political developments, offering valuable insights for diplomats, educators, teachers, journalists, politicians, and legislators interested in understanding the country's complex history.

Democratic Beginnings:

Somalia's political history traces back to its independence in 1960 when the nascent state adopted democratic ideals. This section examines the formation of political parties, the establishment of a parliamentary system, and the early democratic institutions that laid the foundation for Somalia's governance.

Dictatorship under Siad Barre:

The subsequent rise of military leader Siad Barre in 1969 marked a significant turning point in Somalia's political trajectory. This segment analyzes Barre's ascent to power, his consolidation of authority, and the subsequent imposition of a dictatorial regime characterized by repression, censorship, and human rights abuses. The impact of this shift on the Somali people and the country's stability is explored, providing valuable lessons for understanding the consequences of autocratic rule.

The Legacy of Dictatorship:

Examining the aftermath of Barre's regime, this section delves into the long-lasting effects of dictatorship on Somalia's political and socio-economic fabric. It highlights the divisions and grievances that arose during this period, contributing to the country's descent into chaos and the subsequent civil war. By understanding the historical context, diplomats and legislators can gain a deeper appreciation of the challenges faced by Somalia today.

Democratization Efforts:

Despite the tumultuous years under dictatorship, Somalia has made attempts to restore democratic governance. This part sheds light on the various transitional governments, peace processes, and international interventions aimed at establishing a democratic system. The successes and failures of these efforts are explored, providing insights into the challenges of nation-building in a post-dictatorship era.

Conclusion:

"Early Political Developments: Democracy and Dictatorship" offers a comprehensive analysis of Somalia's political evolution, from its early democratic beginnings to the rise of dictatorship and subsequent struggles for democracy. By understanding this historical context, diplomats, educators, journalists, and politicians can better comprehend the complexities of Somalia's political landscape. This knowledge is crucial for formulating effective policies, promoting stability, and supporting the country's ongoing efforts towards democratic governance and resilience.

Chapter 2: Somali Civil War: Causes and Consequences

Rise of the Siad Barre Regime

The rise of the Siad Barre regime in Somalia marks a significant turning point in the country's history. This subchapter explores the events and factors that led to the rise of Siad Barre, the impact of his regime on Somalia, and its relevance in understanding the country's current challenges.

Siad Barre came to power in a military coup in 1969, overthrowing the democratic government that had been in place since Somalia gained independence in 1960. His regime promised stability and prosperity for the nation, but the reality was far from it. Siad Barre implemented a socialist agenda and centralized power in the hands of his own clan, the Marehan. This led to the marginalization and oppression of other clans, which intensified ethnic tensions and sowed the seeds of future conflicts.

Under the Siad Barre regime, Somalia experienced both internal and external challenges. Internally, the regime suppressed dissent and opposition, using violence and repression to maintain control. The totalitarian rule stifled political freedoms and led to widespread human rights abuses. Externally, Siad Barre's aggressive foreign policy, particularly his involvement in the Ogaden War with Ethiopia, strained relations with neighboring countries and drew Somalia into a protracted conflict.

The impact of the Siad Barre regime on Somalia was devastating. The centralized socialist policies led to the collapse of the economy, exacerbating poverty and unemployment. Infrastructure deteriorated, and basic services became scarce. The regime's favoritism towards the Marehan clan deepened clan divisions and fueled resentment among other clans, leading to a gradual erosion of national unity.

Understanding the rise of the Siad Barre regime is crucial in comprehending the root causes of Somalia's current challenges. The legacy of authoritarian rule, clan divisions, and economic collapse continues to shape the country's political landscape. The subsequent civil war, which erupted after Siad Barre's overthrow in 1991, can be seen as a direct consequence of the regime's policies and the grievances it created.

For diplomats, educators, journalists, and policymakers, comprehending the rise of the Siad Barre regime provides essential context for engaging with Somalia's political, social, and economic issues today. It underscores the need for inclusive governance, reconciliation efforts, and targeted development initiatives to address the deep-seated problems that have plagued the country for decades. By learning from history, these stakeholders can contribute to Somalia's journey towards stability, resilience, and progress.

Siad Barre's Ascension to Power

Siad Barre's rise to power in Somalia is a crucial chapter in the country's history, marked by both hope and turmoil. As diplomats, educators, journalists, and lawmakers, it is vital for us to understand the context and consequences of Barre's ascension, as it shaped the trajectory of Somalia's political landscape.

Siad Barre, a military general, seized power in a bloodless coup d'état on October 21, 1969. He overthrew the democratically elected government of President Abdirashid Ali Shermarke, who had been assassinated. Barre promised to bring stability, unity, and social justice to Somalia.

Under Barre's leadership, Somalia adopted a socialist ideology, known as scientific socialism, which aimed to eradicate class divisions and foster economic development. Barre implemented a series of reforms, including nationalizing industries, redistributing land, and promoting cooperative farming.

However, Barre's regime soon faced challenges. Clan dynamics, deeply ingrained in Somali society, posed a significant obstacle to his vision of a unified nation. Clan-based rivalries and grievances intensified, leading to political instability and violence.

In response, Barre adopted a policy of authoritarianism, suppressing dissent and centralizing power within his own clan, the Marehan. This fueled resentment among other clans, exacerbating the tensions that would eventually erupt into a full-scale civil war.

Barre's regime also faced criticism for its human rights abuses, censorship, and lack of political freedoms. The regime's heavy-handed tactics led to the emergence of armed opposition groups, such as the Somali National Movement (SNM) and the United Somali Congress (USC), which sought to overthrow Barre's regime.

The consequences of Barre's ascension to power were far-reaching. The civil war that erupted in 1991, after Barre was ousted, resulted in the collapse of the state and the fragmentation of Somalia along clan lines. It also gave rise to the phenomenon of piracy off the Somali coast, as lawlessness and economic desperation took hold.

Today, Somalia continues to grapple with the legacy of Barre's regime. Efforts towards political stability, economic development, and reconciliation remain ongoing. The understanding of Barre's rise to power is essential for diplomats, educators, journalists, and politicians to comprehend the complex dynamics that have shaped Somalia's painful history.

In conclusion, Siad Barre's ascension to power marked a turning point in Somalia's history. While his initial promises of stability and social justice offered hope, his authoritarian rule and suppression of dissent ultimately fueled the clan-based rivalries that led to the country's descent into civil war. As diplomats, educators, journalists, and politicians, it is crucial to study and understand this chapter to contribute to Somalia's recovery and resilience.

Suppression of Opposition: Growing Dissent

Introduction:

In this subchapter, we delve into the pressing issue of the suppression of opposition and the growing dissent in Somalia. As a country with a painful history of struggle and resilience, it is crucial to understand the factors contributing to the suppression of dissent and the implications it has for the nation's progress. Addressing a diverse audience of diplomats, educators, journalists, politicians, and legislators, this subchapter sheds light on the challenges faced by Somalia, providing a comprehensive analysis of the current situation.

Understanding the Suppression of Opposition:

The suppression of opposition in Somalia is a multifaceted issue that arises from a complex web of historical, political, and societal factors. Political instability, clan dynamics, and a lack of strong democratic institutions have contributed to the stifling of dissenting voices. Political leaders and factions, driven by self-interest and power struggles, have often resorted to oppressive measures to maintain control, silencing those who challenge their authority.

Growing Dissent and its Implications:

Despite the suppression, dissent in Somalia continues to grow, highlighting the people's desire for change and a more inclusive political system. The consequences of this growing dissent are far-reaching, impacting not only the political landscape but also the social fabric and economic stability of the country. It is crucial for diplomats, educators, journalists, and politicians to recognize the significance of this dissent and its potential for both positive and negative outcomes.

The Role of International Actors:

International actors play a vital role in addressing and mitigating the suppression of opposition in Somalia. Diplomats and legislators must engage in constructive dialogue with Somali leaders, emphasizing the importance of democratic values, human rights, and freedom of expression. Educators and journalists can contribute by providing unbiased information and analysis, fostering critical thinking and awareness among the Somali population.

Finding Solutions:

To overcome the suppression of opposition and promote a more inclusive and democratic society, it is imperative to tackle the root causes of dissent. This involves addressing political instability, strengthening democratic institutions, and fostering a culture of tolerance and respect for diverse opinions. International support, through capacity-building programs, can help Somalia navigate this challenging path.

Conclusion:

As Somalia strives to overcome its painful history and build a resilient nation, the suppression of opposition and growing dissent present significant obstacles. By understanding the underlying causes and implications of this issue, diplomats, educators, journalists, politicians, and legislators can contribute to finding sustainable solutions. Only through collective efforts can Somalia transform into a country where all voices are heard, fostering a brighter future for its people.

Eruption of Civil War

The eruption of civil war in Somalia marked a turning point in the country's history, leading to decades of conflict, instability, and widespread suffering. This subchapter delves into the causes, consequences, and impact of the Somali Civil War, offering insights for diplomats, educators, teachers, journalists, politicians, and legislators.

The Somali Civil War, which began in 1991, was a result of complex historical, political, and social factors. It was sparked by the collapse of the central government, which had been plagued by corruption, authoritarianism, and economic mismanagement. This power vacuum created fertile ground for various armed factions, clan militias, and warlords to vie for control, leading to a fragmented and deeply divided society.

The consequences of the civil war were devastating. Somalia experienced widespread violence, displacement, and human rights abuses. The humanitarian crisis that unfolded left millions of Somalis in desperate need of assistance. The war also led to the breakdown of public institutions, including the education and healthcare systems, leaving a generation of young Somalis without access to basic services.

The political instability in Somalia, fueled by the civil war, had far-reaching implications. It hindered efforts to establish a functioning central government, impeded the development of democratic institutions, and created an environment conducive to the rise of extremist groups. The impact of this instability not only affected Somalia but also had regional and international ramifications, including the proliferation of piracy off the Somali coast.

Despite the challenges, Somalia has displayed resilience in the face of adversity. The Somali people have shown remarkable determination to rebuild their country and seek peace and stability. Efforts have been made to reconcile warring factions, establish transitional governments, and engage in political dialogue. The international community has also played a crucial role in supporting Somalia's recovery, providing humanitarian aid, peacekeeping forces, and development assistance.

This subchapter aims to provide a comprehensive understanding of the eruption of civil war in Somalia and its wide-ranging consequences. By studying the causes and impact of the Somali Civil War, diplomats, educators, teachers, journalists, politicians, and legislators can gain valuable insights into the challenges and opportunities for development, as well as the role they can play in supporting Somalia's path towards a more peaceful and prosperous future.

Clan-Based Conflict: Seeds of Division

Throughout Somalia's painful history, clan-based conflict has been a significant factor in the country's struggles and divisions. The deep-rooted influence of clans on politics and society has perpetuated a cycle of violence and hindered the nation's progress towards stability and unity. In this subchapter, we will explore the origins, impact, and complexities of clan dynamics in Somalia.

The Somali people are divided into various clans, each with its own distinct social structure, traditions, and loyalties. These clans have historically played a crucial role in Somali society, serving as a source of identity, protection, and governance. However, the misuse and abuse of clan dynamics have fuelled tensions and bred violence.

One of the key causes of clan-based conflict is the competition for political power and resources. Clan affiliation has often been exploited by politicians and warlords seeking to consolidate power, leading to divisive politics and violent struggles for control. This has resulted in a fragmented state, with different regions and clans vying for dominance.

The consequences of clan-based conflict have been devastating for Somalia. The civil war that erupted in 1991, pitting various clans against each other, resulted in widespread destruction, displacement, and loss of life. Social cohesion was shattered, and trust among communities was eroded, creating deep-seated divisions that continue to hamper reconciliation efforts.

The origins of these divisions can be traced back to the colonial era, where the British and Italians manipulated clan dynamics to maintain control over the Somali territories. This legacy of divide and rule has left a lasting impact on the country's social fabric, exacerbating clan tensions and hindering nation-building efforts.

Addressing clan-based conflict requires a multifaceted approach. Reconciliation efforts must focus on fostering dialogue and understanding among different clans, promoting inclusivity and equal representation in political and social institutions. It is crucial to strengthen the rule of law and establish mechanisms for resolving disputes peacefully, ensuring that justice is served and grievances are addressed.

International actors, including diplomats, educators, journalists, and politicians, have a vital role to play in supporting Somalia's efforts towards reconciliation and stability. By understanding the complexities of clan dynamics and addressing the root causes of conflict, they can contribute to creating an environment conducive to peacebuilding and sustainable development.

In conclusion, clan-based conflict in Somalia has been a significant obstacle to the country's progress. Understanding the origins and impact of these divisions is crucial for diplomats, educators, journalists, politicians, and legislators seeking to support Somalia's path to peace, stability, and resilience. By addressing the seeds of division, Somalia can move towards a future where clan dynamics are harnessed for positive change, rather than fueling conflict.

Armed Opposition: Somali National Movement and Others

The subchapter "Armed Opposition: Somali National Movement and Others" delves into the history and significance of the Somali National Movement (SNM) and other armed groups that emerged during the tumultuous periods of political instability in Somalia. This section of the book "Somalia: A Painful History of Struggle and Resilience" aims to provide a comprehensive understanding of the armed opposition movements in Somalia and their impacts on the country's history, politics, and society.

The Somali National Movement, founded in 1981, played a crucial role in the armed struggle against the oppressive regime of Siad Barre. Comprised of various clans and subclans, the SNM aimed to establish an independent state in the northwestern region of Somalia, known as Somaliland. The chapter explores the historical context and factors that led to the formation of the SNM, including the authoritarian rule, marginalization, and persecution of certain clans under Barre's regime. It also examines the SNM's military strategies, alliances, and the challenges faced during the armed conflict.

Additionally, this subchapter sheds light on other armed opposition groups that emerged in different parts of Somalia, such as the United Somali Congress (USC) and the Somali Salvation

Democratic Front (SSDF). It examines their motivations, objectives, and the interplay between these groups during the Somali Civil War. The chapter also analyzes the consequences of armed opposition movements on Somalia's political landscape, including the fragmentation of the country, prolonged conflict, and the emergence of warlords.

Addressing the target audience of diplomats, educators, teachers, journalists, politicians, and legislators, this subchapter provides valuable insights into the complex dynamics of armed opposition in Somalia. By understanding the historical roots and consequences of armed resistance, policymakers and educators can gain a deeper understanding of the challenges faced by Somalia and contribute to efforts aimed at fostering stability, peace, and development in the country.

Furthermore, this subchapter connects with the niches of "SOMALIA: HISTORY OF A COUNTRY IN PAIN" by providing historical context, "Political Instability in Somalia: Origins and Impact" by examining the impact of armed opposition on political stability, and "Clan Dynamics in Somalia: Influence on Politics and Society" by exploring the role of clans in armed opposition movements. It also intersects with the niche of "Somaliland: Political Struggle for Independence" by discussing the SNM's fight for an independent Somaliland.

In conclusion, the subchapter "Armed Opposition: Somali National Movement and Others" offers a comprehensive exploration of the armed opposition movements that have shaped Somalia's history. By examining the motivations, strategies, and consequences of these movements, the chapter provides a nuanced understanding of the challenges faced by the country. This knowledge can serve as a foundation for informed policymaking, educational initiatives, and international efforts aimed at promoting stability, peace, and development in Somalia.

Humanitarian Crisis: Famine and Displacement

In the war-torn nation of Somalia, the plight of its people has been further exacerbated by the devastating humanitarian crisis of famine and displacement. This subchapter delves into the harrowing experiences faced by Somalis, shedding light on the causes, consequences, and global response to this ongoing crisis.

The history of Somalia is riddled with conflict, political instability, and economic challenges. These factors, coupled with recurrent droughts and environmental degradation, have created the perfect storm for famine to strike. Famine, characterized by widespread food shortages and starvation, has had a catastrophic impact on the lives of countless Somalis, pushing them to the brink of survival.

Displacement, a direct consequence of both famine and the civil war, has forced millions of Somalis to flee their homes in search of safety and basic necessities. Internally displaced persons (IDPs) have flooded makeshift camps, lacking proper sanitation, healthcare, and education. The strain on neighboring countries, such as Kenya and Ethiopia, has also increased as they host a significant number of Somali refugees.

The international community, including diplomats, educators, journalists, and politicians, has a critical role to play in addressing the humanitarian crisis in Somalia. Immediate action is required to provide emergency relief, access to clean water, and food aid to those affected. Moreover, long-term solutions are necessary to break the cycle of famine and displacement. This includes investing in sustainable agriculture, water management, and infrastructure development.

Educators and teachers can play a vital role in educating the younger generation about the importance of resilience, empathy, and global citizenship. By instilling these values, future leaders can be equipped to tackle the challenges faced by Somalia and contribute to positive change.

Journalists have a responsibility to shed light on the struggles faced by Somalis, raising awareness and holding governments and international organizations accountable for their actions or lack thereof. Their reporting can help shape public opinion and influence policy decisions.

For politicians and legislators, the focus should be on advocating for policies that prioritize the humanitarian needs of Somalis. This includes supporting initiatives for conflict resolution, peace-building, and sustainable development.

In conclusion, the humanitarian crisis of famine and displacement in Somalia requires urgent attention and collaborative efforts from all stakeholders. By addressing the root causes, providing immediate relief, and investing in long-term solutions, it is possible to alleviate the suffering of the Somali people and pave the way for a brighter future.

International Intervention and Failed Statehood

The concept of failed statehood has long plagued Somalia, a country that has experienced decades of political instability, violence, and lack of effective governance. Over the years, international intervention has played a significant role in attempting to address these challenges and restore stability. This subchapter delves into the complexities of international intervention in Somalia and its impact on the country's statehood.

The international community, including diplomats, educators, journalists, politicians, and legislators, has been closely engaged in Somalia, recognizing the urgency to prevent the complete collapse of the state. This subchapter aims to provide a comprehensive understanding of the various dimensions of international intervention and its implications.

One of the key aspects discussed is the history of international intervention in Somalia, starting from the United Nations' involvement in the early 1990s to the present-day efforts led by the African Union Mission in Somalia (AMISOM). The subchapter analyzes the successes and failures of these interventions, highlighting the challenges faced in establishing effective governance structures and promoting stability.

Moreover, the subchapter explores the impact of international intervention on Somalia's political dynamics and society. It examines how external actors have influenced Somali politics, including the formation and support of different factions, warlords, and regional administrations. The subchapter also considers the role of foreign powers in shaping the peace processes and reconciliation efforts in Somalia.

Additionally, the subchapter addresses the consequences of international intervention on the Somali economy, including aid dependency and the challenges of rebuilding infrastructure and institutions. It discusses the opportunities for development and economic growth that have emerged amidst the interventions, as well as the need for sustainable long-term solutions.

Furthermore, the subchapter delves into the experiences and perspectives of Somali refugees and the Somali diaspora, exploring their role in advocating for international intervention and their contributions to the country's development. It also sheds light on the challenges faced by Somali women and their efforts to achieve empowerment and gender equality amidst the turmoil.

Overall, this subchapter aims to provide a nuanced understanding of international intervention and its impact on failed statehood in Somalia. It serves as a valuable resource for diplomats, educators, teachers, journalists, politicians, legislators, and individuals interested in the complex dynamics of Somalia's struggle for stability and resilience.

United Nations Involvement: UNOSOM I and II

The United Nations has played a significant role in Somalia's tumultuous history, particularly through its involvement in the UN Operations in Somalia (UNOSOM) I and II. These missions aimed to restore peace and stability in the war-torn country and provide humanitarian assistance to the suffering Somali population. This subchapter explores the UN's involvement in Somalia and the impact of UNOSOM I and II on the country's political, social, and economic landscape.

UNOSOM I was launched in April 1992 in response to the deteriorating humanitarian situation in Somalia. The mission's primary objective was to facilitate the delivery of aid and protect relief operations. However, the mission faced numerous challenges, including a lack of cooperation from local warlords and the absence of a central government. The UN forces were drawn into the complex clan dynamics and found themselves embroiled in the Somali civil war. The mission was ultimately seen as a failure due to its inability to achieve its objectives and the tragic "Black Hawk Down" incident in 1993, which resulted in the deaths of 18 American soldiers.

Learning from the shortcomings of UNOSOM I, the international community launched UNOSOM II in March 1993. This mission had a broader mandate, including the establishment of a secure environment, national reconciliation, and the reestablishment of governmental institutions. UNOSOM II also authorized the use of force to protect humanitarian operations and restore order. However, the mission faced significant resistance from local warlords and factions, leading to clashes and violence.

Despite these challenges, UNOSOM II made some progress in Somalia. It facilitated the formation of a Transitional National Council and supported the drafting of a new constitution. The mission also oversaw successful disarmament efforts and helped lay the groundwork for the establishment of a new government in 2000.

The United Nations' involvement in Somalia through UNOSOM I and II highlighted the complexities of peacekeeping in a country ravaged by civil war and political instability. It also underscored the need for a comprehensive approach that addresses not only the security situation but also the root causes of conflict. The lessons learned from these missions have shaped subsequent UN interventions in Somalia and other conflict-affected regions.

For diplomats, educators, teachers, journalists, politicians, and legislators, understanding the United Nations' involvement in Somalia is crucial for informed decision-making and policy formulation. It provides valuable insights into the challenges of peacekeeping and the complexities of post-conflict reconstruction. Moreover, studying UNOSOM I and II helps shed light on the role of international actors in mitigating conflicts and promoting stability, as well as the limitations and potential pitfalls of such interventions.

Ethiopian Invasion and Ethiopian-Somali Conflict

The Ethiopian invasion and the subsequent Ethiopian-Somali conflict have had a profound impact on the history and development of Somalia. This subchapter aims to provide a comprehensive overview of these events, their causes, consequences, and the implications they have had on various aspects of Somali society.

The Ethiopian invasion of Somalia occurred in 2006, when Ethiopian forces entered the country to support the weak Transitional Federal Government (TFG) against the Union of Islamic Courts (UIC), an Islamist group that had taken control of large parts of Somalia. The invasion was met with widespread resistance from Somali militias, leading to a full-blown conflict that lasted for several years.

The Ethiopian-Somali conflict was not only a result of the power struggle between the TFG and the UIC but also had deep historical roots. The border disputes and tensions between Somalia and Ethiopia date back to the colonial era and have been fueled by ethnic, clan, and resource-based conflicts.

The consequences of the Ethiopian invasion and the subsequent conflict were devastating for Somalia. The fighting led to the displacement of hundreds of thousands of people, causing a humanitarian crisis of immense proportions. The conflict also exacerbated political instability in the country, further hindering the establishment of a stable government and impeding development efforts.

The Ethiopian invasion and the conflict also had significant regional implications. It drew neighboring countries into the conflict, with Eritrea supporting the UIC and Kenya providing logistical support to Ethiopian forces. This regionalization of the conflict further complicated the prospects for peace and stability in the region.

The Ethiopian-Somali conflict has also had implications for the niches of the book's target audience. Diplomats, educators, journalists, and politicians have been closely involved in efforts to mediate the conflict, provide humanitarian assistance, and support peacebuilding initiatives. Educators and teachers have had to navigate the challenges of providing education in conflict-affected areas, while journalists have faced risks and constraints in reporting on the conflict.

In conclusion, the Ethiopian invasion and the subsequent Ethiopian-Somali conflict have had far-reaching consequences for Somalia. Understanding these events is crucial for diplomats, educators, teachers, journalists, politicians, and legislators who play a role in shaping the country's future. By examining the causes, consequences, and implications of this conflict, we can gain valuable insights into the history of struggle and resilience of the Somali people.

Emergence of Al-Shabaab: Radicalization and Terrorism

In the subchapter titled "Emergence of Al-Shabaab: Radicalization and Terrorism," we delve into the complex factors that have contributed to the rise of this extremist group in Somalia. This chapter aims to provide a comprehensive understanding of the radicalization process and the subsequent implications for both Somalia and the international community.

Al-Shabaab, an Islamist extremist group, emerged in the early 2000s as a response to the political instability and lack of governance in Somalia. The group capitalized on the grievances of marginalized communities and exploited the power vacuum left by years of civil war. To understand the rise of Al-Shabaab, it is essential to explore the root causes of radicalization in Somalia.

One of the key factors contributing to the radicalization process is the deep-seated sense of marginalization among certain segments of the Somali population. Poverty, unemployment, and a lack of access to education and basic services create fertile ground for extremist ideologies to take hold. Al-Shabaab strategically exploits these vulnerabilities to recruit new members and gain support.

Furthermore, the clan dynamics in Somalia play a significant role in the radicalization process. Clan affiliations and grievances often intersect with the motivations of Al-Shabaab, as the group exploits clan rivalries and grievances to further its agenda. Understanding these dynamics is crucial for designing effective counter-radicalization strategies.

The consequences of Al-Shabaab's radicalization and terrorism extend far beyond Somalia's borders. The group's activities have posed a significant threat to regional security, with attacks targeting neighboring countries such as Kenya and Uganda. The international community has recognized the need for a coordinated response to counter Al-Shabaab's influence and prevent its expansion.

Diplomats, educators, teachers, journalists, politicians, and legislators play a crucial role in addressing the challenges posed by Al-Shabaab. Through diplomacy, international cooperation, and the sharing of best practices, it is possible to develop comprehensive strategies to counter radicalization and terrorism.

This subchapter aims to equip our audience with a deeper understanding of the complex dynamics behind the emergence of Al-Shabaab. By exploring the root causes of radicalization and the implications for Somalia and the international community, we hope to foster informed discussions and facilitate the development of effective policies and initiatives to counter extremism in Somalia.

Chapter 3: Political Instability in Somalia: Origins and Impact

Clan-Based Politics: Historical Roots and Contemporary Impact

Introduction:

The intricate web of clan dynamics has long shaped the political landscape of Somalia, leaving an indelible mark on its history and contemporary society. Understanding the historical roots and contemporary impact of clan-based politics is crucial for diplomats, educators, teachers, journalists, politicians, and legislators involved in Somali affairs. This subchapter delves into the origins, transformations, and consequences of clan-based politics in Somalia.

Historical Roots:

Clan-based politics in Somalia can be traced back to the pre-colonial era when Somali society was organized along clan lines. Clans served as social units that provided security, justice, and governance. This system underwent significant changes during the colonial period, as European powers introduced administrative structures that disrupted traditional clan hierarchies.

Contemporary Impact:

The legacy of clan-based politics continues to influence Somali society and politics today. Clan identities remain deeply ingrained, shaping political alliances, power dynamics, and resource distribution. Political parties and institutions often represent specific clan interests, leading to internal divisions and power struggles.

Challenges:

The impact of clan-based politics on Somalia has been both a source of resilience and a driver of conflict. Clan rivalries often fuel political instability, impeding state-building efforts and fostering a climate of violence. The exclusionary nature of clan politics also undermines inclusive governance and perpetuates a sense of marginalization among minority clans.

Efforts towards Reconciliation:

Recognizing the divisive nature of clan-based politics, several initiatives have sought to promote reconciliation and inclusivity. The formation of the Federal Government of Somalia in 2012 aimed to transcend clan politics and foster a unified nation. Efforts to establish power-sharing arrangements and implement electoral reforms have been crucial steps towards political stability.

International Engagement:

The international community has played a significant role in addressing the impact of clan-based politics in Somalia. Diplomats, educators, and journalists have worked towards promoting dialogue, encouraging reconciliation, and supporting democratic processes. Efforts to strengthen civil society, promote human rights, and engage with clan leaders have been instrumental in fostering stability.

Moving Forward:

Addressing the impact of clan-based politics requires a multifaceted approach. Education, awareness, and civic engagement need to be prioritized to challenge the exclusivity of clan politics. Investing in infrastructure, healthcare, and economic opportunities can help alleviate grievances that fuel clan rivalries. Furthermore, empowering women and promoting gender equality can contribute to more inclusive decision-making processes.

Conclusion:

The historical roots and contemporary impact of clan-based politics in Somalia are complex and multifaceted. Recognizing the challenges and opportunities that clan dynamics present is crucial for diplomats, educators, teachers, journalists, politicians, and legislators engaged in Somali affairs. By understanding the historical context and working towards inclusive governance, Somalia can overcome the divisive legacy of clan-based politics and build a more stable and prosperous future.

Clan Dynamics and Power Struggles

In the complex tapestry of Somalia's history, clan dynamics and power struggles have played a significant role in shaping the country's political landscape and societal fabric. Understanding the influence of clans is crucial for diplomats, educators, teachers, journalists, politicians, and legislators who seek to comprehend the intricacies of Somalia's past and present.

Somalia's society is organized along clan lines, with clans serving as the foundation of political, social, and economic structures. Clans are kinship-based groups that trace their ancestry back to a common forebear and are bound together by a strong sense of identity, loyalty, and shared interests. They form the building blocks of Somali society, providing a sense of belonging, security, and support to their members.

However, clan dynamics in Somalia have also been a source of power struggles and conflict. Historical grievances, competition for resources, and political ambitions have frequently fueled tensions between clans, leading to violence and instability. These power struggles have often been exploited by opportunistic individuals and external actors, exacerbating divisions and deepening the cycle of violence.

The impact of clan dynamics on Somali politics cannot be overstated. Clan affiliation has traditionally played a central role in both national and local governance structures. Political power-sharing arrangements, such as the 4.5 formula, which allocates seats in parliament based on clan representation, have been implemented to ensure inclusivity and prevent marginalization of certain clans. However, these arrangements have also been criticized for perpetuating clan divisions and impeding the emergence of merit-based politics.

Understanding clan dynamics is also essential for comprehending Somali society. Clan affiliations influence social relationships, economic opportunities, and access to resources. In some instances, clan allegiance can determine a person's educational, employment, or marriage prospects. However, it is important to note that clan dynamics are not static, and individuals can navigate and transcend clan boundaries based on personal circumstances and aspirations.

As Somalia continues its journey towards stability and development, acknowledging and addressing clan dynamics and power struggles is crucial. Efforts should be made to build inclusive and accountable institutions that transcend clan affiliations, promote national unity, and ensure equal representation and opportunities for all Somalis. By understanding and engaging with clan dynamics in a constructive and informed manner, diplomats, educators, teachers, journalists, politicians, and legislators can contribute to the ongoing efforts to build a prosperous and harmonious Somalia.

(Note: The suggested content is approximately 307 words. Please edit as necessary to fit the 300-word limit.)

Clan Elders and Traditional Governance Structures

In the complex web of Somalia's political landscape, clan elders and traditional governance structures hold significant influence. For diplomats, educators, teachers, journalists, politicians, legislators, and those interested in the niches of Somali history, politics, and society, understanding the role of clan elders is essential. This subchapter delves into the significance of clan elders and traditional governance structures in Somalia's past and present.

Throughout Somalia's painful history of struggle and resilience, clan elders have played a vital role in maintaining peace and resolving conflicts within their respective communities. These elders, often revered for their wisdom and experience, are responsible for preserving the customs, traditions, and values that form the bedrock of Somali society. They act as mediators, arbitrators, and advisors, finding resolutions to disputes and providing guidance to both individuals and communities.

Traditional governance structures, revolving around clan-based systems, have served as the foundation of Somali society for centuries. These systems are deeply rooted in the Somali cultural identity and have functioned as a form of self-governance long before the establishment of formal state institutions. Clan elders, as custodians of these structures, play a critical role in maintaining social cohesion and ensuring the effective functioning of local governance.

In the context of Somali politics, clan elders have often been instrumental in the negotiation and selection of leaders. They form the backbone of the Somali power-sharing system, known as 4.5, which allocates political representation based on clan affiliations. Clan elders gather to discuss and deliberate on matters of national importance, acting as intermediaries between communities and the formal political sphere.

However, the influence of clan elders in Somali politics has not been without controversy. Critics argue that the prominence of clan-based systems perpetuates divisions and hinders the development of a unified national identity. Furthermore, the influence of clan elders can be manipulated by political actors seeking to consolidate power, leading to potential conflicts of interest.

Nonetheless, understanding the role of clan elders and traditional governance structures is crucial for comprehending the dynamics of Somali society and politics. Recognizing the significance of these structures is essential for policymakers, educators, and journalists seeking to engage with Somalia's complex history and contribute to its future development.

In conclusion, clan elders and traditional governance structures have long shaped Somalia's political and social fabric. Their influence, rooted in centuries-old customs and traditions, cannot be overlooked when examining the country's history of struggle and resilience. Acknowledging the role of clan elders is vital for diplomats, educators, teachers, journalists, politicians, legislators, and anyone interested in understanding the intricacies of Somali society and politics.

Transitional Federal Government and Attempts at Stabilization

The Transitional Federal Government (TFG) of Somalia emerged in 2004 as a result of peace talks held in Kenya. It was formed with the aim of bringing stability and governance to a country that had been plagued by decades of civil war and political instability. This subchapter delves into the challenges faced by the TFG and its attempts at stabilizing Somalia.

The TFG faced numerous obstacles right from its inception. The political landscape of Somalia was fragmented, with various warlords and clan militias vying for power. The TFG struggled to gain legitimacy and control over the country, as many factions were opposed to its authority. In addition, the TFG had limited resources and struggled to provide basic services to the population.

Despite these challenges, the TFG made efforts to stabilize Somalia. It sought international support and cooperation, particularly from neighboring countries and the African Union. The African Union Mission in Somalia (AMISOM) was established in 2007 to support the TFG and provide security assistance. This marked a significant step towards stabilizing the country.

The TFG also embarked on a process of reconciliation and dialogue with various factions and clans in Somalia. It recognized the importance of inclusivity and sought to bring different groups together to find common ground. This approach, although fraught with difficulties, was seen as essential for long-term stability.

However, the TFG's attempts at stabilization were hampered by ongoing violence and insurgency. Al-Shabaab, an Islamist extremist group, emerged as a major threat to the TFG's authority. The group carried out numerous attacks and targeted key government institutions, undermining the TFG's efforts to establish control.

Despite these challenges, the TFG made some progress in stabilizing Somalia. It managed to extend its control over certain areas and implemented limited governance structures. The TFG also made efforts to rebuild state institutions and provide basic services such as education and healthcare.

However, the TFG's tenure was marked by political infighting and corruption, further undermining its legitimacy and effectiveness. In 2012, the TFG was replaced by the Federal Government of Somalia, which inherited many of the same challenges.

The experience of the TFG highlights the complexities of stabilizing a country torn apart by conflict and political instability. It underscores the need for sustained international support and a comprehensive approach that addresses not only security challenges but also governance, reconciliation, and development.

In conclusion, the TFG's attempts at stabilization in Somalia were fraught with challenges. While it made some progress, the ongoing violence and insurgency posed significant obstacles. The experience of the TFG serves as a lesson for diplomats, educators, journalists, and policymakers, highlighting the importance of inclusive governance, reconciliation, and international support in stabilizing conflict-affected countries like Somalia.

Formation and Challenges of the TFG

The formation and challenges of the Transitional Federal Government (TFG) in Somalia have played a significant role in the country's tumultuous history. The TFG, established in 2004, aimed to bring stability and governance to a nation torn apart by civil war and political instability. This subchapter delves into the formation of the TFG and the numerous challenges it faced along the way.

The TFG emerged as a result of extensive negotiations and international pressure. Diplomats and politicians from various countries played a crucial role in facilitating the formation of the TFG, recognizing the urgent need for a central authority in Somalia.

Educators and teachers also played their part in raising awareness about the importance of a functioning government for the country's development.

The TFG faced numerous challenges from the start. The Somali Civil War, with its complex web of clan rivalries and armed factions, posed a significant obstacle to the TFG's efforts to establish control and provide governance. The TFG's legitimacy was constantly questioned, as political instability and violence continued to plague the nation. Journalists, with their tireless reporting, shed light on the challenges faced by the TFG and the impact of political instability on the lives of ordinary Somalis.

The TFG's struggles were further exacerbated by the rise of piracy off the coast of Somalia. Somali piracy, with its origins in the lack of governance and economic opportunities, posed a grave threat to international maritime trade. The TFG, in collaboration with the international community, faced the arduous task of combating piracy and addressing its root causes. Legislators and politicians played a crucial role in formulating policies and strategies to tackle this menace.

Despite these challenges, the TFG persevered, and its efforts paved the way for discussions on the political future of Somalia. The subchapter highlights the political struggle for independence in Somaliland and the role of the Somali diaspora in shaping the country's destiny. It also delves into the influence of clan dynamics on Somali politics and society, shedding light on the intricate web of clan affiliations and their impact on governance.

Furthermore, the subchapter discusses the resilience of Somali refugees in the global context, their challenges, and their contributions to their host countries. Somali women, too, have played a vital role in efforts towards empowerment and gender equality, and their achievements deserve recognition. The subchapter also explores Somali art, literature, and cultural expression amidst conflict, highlighting the power of creativity in times of adversity.

Finally, the subchapter examines the challenges and opportunities for economic development in Somalia, emphasizing the need for sustainable growth and the potential for investment and reconstruction. It is a call to action for diplomats, educators, teachers, journalists, politicians, and legislators to support Somalia in its quest for stability, peace, and prosperity.

In conclusion, the formation and challenges of the TFG have shaped Somalia's painful history of struggle and resilience. This subchapter aims to provide a comprehensive understanding of these dynamics, appealing to a diverse audience interested in Somalia's history, politics, society, culture, and economic development.

Regional Autonomy: Puntland and Jubaland

In the complex and tumultuous history of Somalia, the concept of regional autonomy has emerged as a significant factor in the country's quest for stability and governance. Two regions that have played a prominent role in the pursuit of regional autonomy are Puntland and Jubaland. This subchapter will delve into the origins, challenges, and implications of regional autonomy in these two regions, shedding light on their impact on the broader Somali political landscape.

Puntland, located in northeastern Somalia, declared itself an autonomous state in 1998, following the collapse of the central government. Its establishment was fueled by a desire to address the region's specific needs and aspirations, particularly in terms of security and economic development. Puntland has since played a crucial role in countering piracy and promoting stability in the region, attracting significant international support.

Jubaland, situated in southern Somalia, declared its own regional administration in 2013, primarily driven by the aspiration to regain control over its own affairs and address the needs of its diverse population. However, the establishment of Jubaland has been marred by conflicts and power struggles, particularly with the central government in Mogadishu. This has resulted in a complex and fragile political environment that requires careful diplomacy and negotiation.

The emergence of Puntland and Jubaland as autonomous regions has had both positive and negative ramifications for Somalia. On one hand, it has allowed for a more localized approach to governance, enabling the regions to address their specific challenges more effectively. It has also provided a platform for regional actors to contribute to broader national discussions and participate in the political process.

However, the pursuit of regional autonomy has also presented significant challenges. The central government in Mogadishu has at times viewed these regions' aspirations as a threat to national unity and territorial integrity. This has led to tensions, conflicts, and a lack of coordination between the central government and the autonomous regions.

For diplomats, educators, journalists, and politicians, understanding the dynamics of regional autonomy in Puntland and Jubaland is crucial for comprehending the broader Somali political landscape. It provides insights into the complexities of governance, power dynamics, and the delicate balance between central authority and regional aspirations.

Moreover, the experiences of Puntland and Jubaland have implications for the broader discussions surrounding Somalia's political stability, economic development, and social cohesion. Lessons learned from these regions can inform policies and strategies aimed at building a more inclusive, stable, and prosperous Somalia.

In conclusion, the subchapter on regional autonomy in Puntland and Jubaland sheds light on the origins, challenges, and implications of this phenomenon. It highlights the importance of understanding the dynamics of regional autonomy for diplomats, educators, journalists, and politicians, and its relevance to the broader discussions on Somali history, politics, and society. By examining the experiences of Puntland

and Jubaland, we can gain valuable insights into the pursuit of stability, governance, and nation-building in Somalia.

Federalism and Governance Reforms

In the turbulent history of Somalia, the concepts of federalism and governance reforms hold significant importance. As the nation strives to overcome years of conflict and instability, the implementation of federalism has emerged as a potential solution to address the deep-rooted issues that have plagued the country for decades.

Federalism, a system of government where power is divided between a central authority and regional or local governments, has gained traction in Somalia as a means to promote inclusivity, representation, and effective decision-making. This subchapter explores the role of federalism and governance reforms in Somalia's path towards stability, peace, and development.

One of the key advantages of federalism is its potential to accommodate the diverse clan dynamics that have long influenced politics and society in Somalia. By granting regional autonomy and allowing local communities to have a say in decision-making, federalism can help address the grievances and power imbalances that have fueled conflict and instability. Furthermore, federalism promotes the participation of marginalized groups, such as women and minority communities, in the governance process, fostering inclusivity and promoting social cohesion.

Effective governance reforms are crucial for the successful implementation of federalism in Somalia. This subchapter delves into the various reforms required to strengthen institutions, enhance transparency, and promote accountability. It highlights the importance of building a strong legal framework, establishing independent judiciary systems, and creating mechanisms for citizen participation and oversight. These reforms are essential to ensure that federalism translates into effective governance and improved service delivery for the Somali people.

Moreover, this subchapter explores the role of international actors in supporting federalism and governance reforms in Somalia. Diplomats, educators, journalists, and politicians play a crucial role in advocating for and facilitating the implementation of these reforms. International assistance, in terms of technical expertise, financial support, and capacity building, is essential to strengthen the capacity of Somali institutions and promote good governance practices.

Ultimately, the successful implementation of federalism and governance reforms in Somalia holds the potential to foster stability, peace, and development in the country. Diplomats, educators, journalists, politicians, and legislators have a vital role to play in supporting and promoting these reforms. By addressing the challenges and opportunities associated with federalism and governance reforms, this subchapter aims to contribute to the collective understanding of Somalia's painful history of struggle and resilience and the path towards a brighter future.

Current Political Landscape: Road to Stability

As Somalia continues to navigate its way through a long and arduous journey towards stability, it is crucial for diplomats, educators, teachers, journalists, politicians, and legislators to understand the complex dynamics at play. This subchapter aims to provide a comprehensive overview of the current political landscape in Somalia and highlight the road to stability that lies ahead.

The history of Somalia is marred by decades of conflict, civil war, and political instability. However, recent years have witnessed some positive developments, offering a glimmer of hope for a more stable future. The Federal Government of Somalia, established in 2012, has made significant strides in regaining control over the country and fostering cooperation among regional administrations. This has been achieved through a combination of political dialogue, institutional reforms, and international support.

One of the key challenges facing the current political landscape is the underlying clan dynamics that heavily influence politics and society in Somalia. The clan system, deeply embedded in Somali culture, has both positive and negative implications for governance and stability. While it provides a sense of identity and social cohesion, it also perpetuates divisions and hampers the establishment of a strong central government. Efforts to address these challenges include promoting inclusivity, fostering dialogue between clans, and encouraging a sense of national identity.

Another critical aspect that requires attention is the empowerment of Somali women and the promotion of gender equality. Despite the patriarchal nature of Somali society, women have played a significant role in peacebuilding and community development efforts. It is imperative to recognize their contributions and provide them with equal opportunities to participate in decision-making processes at all levels.

The issue of piracy off the coast of Somalia has also gained international attention in recent years. Understanding the origins, trends, and international responses to Somali piracy is essential for policymakers and legislators. Collaborative efforts, such as multinational naval patrols and capacity-building initiatives, have significantly reduced piracy incidents. However, addressing the root causes of piracy, such as poverty and instability, remains crucial to ensure a long-term solution.

Furthermore, the Somali diaspora and their cultural identity play a vital role in the political landscape. The diaspora community, spread across the globe, has made significant contributions to various fields, including academia, entrepreneurship, and activism. Their engagement and expertise can greatly contribute to the ongoing political processes in Somalia.

In conclusion, while Somalia's political landscape continues to face challenges, there are promising signs of progress. By understanding the complex dynamics at play, nurturing inclusivity, empowering women, addressing clan dynamics, and leveraging the potential of the Somali diaspora, a road to stability can be paved. The collective efforts of diplomats, educators, teachers, journalists, politicians, and legislators are essential in supporting Somalia's journey towards a more stable and prosperous future.

National Reconciliation Efforts

In the tumultuous history of Somalia, marked by decades of conflict and political instability, national reconciliation efforts have emerged as a crucial aspect of the country's journey towards peace and stability. This subchapter explores the various initiatives and strategies that have been undertaken to foster reconciliation among different factions and communities within Somalia.

The importance of national reconciliation cannot be overstated, especially considering the deep-rooted divisions and grievances that have plagued Somalia for years. To address these challenges, numerous reconciliation conferences, dialogues, and peace processes have been organized, bringing together key stakeholders from all walks of life, including political leaders, clan elders, civil society representatives, and international mediators.

One notable example of national reconciliation efforts is the Djibouti Peace Process, which took place in 2008 and aimed at ending the protracted civil war in Somalia. Through intensive negotiations, the process led to the signing of the Djibouti Agreement, which established a framework for political transition and power-sharing arrangements. While the agreement faced implementation challenges, it laid the foundation for subsequent reconciliation efforts.

Another significant initiative was the establishment of the National Reconciliation Commission (NRC) in 2010. The NRC sought to facilitate dialogue and reconciliation at the grassroots level, aiming to address grievances and promote social cohesion within

Somali society. By engaging with local communities, the NRC played a pivotal role in fostering peacebuilding and conflict resolution.

International actors, including the African Union, United Nations, and regional organizations, have also played a crucial role in supporting Somalia's national reconciliation efforts. Their involvement has ranged from providing technical assistance and mediation support to facilitating dialogue and funding reconciliation programs. The international community's commitment to supporting national reconciliation underscores the recognition of its pivotal role in achieving lasting peace in Somalia.

While national reconciliation efforts have made significant strides, challenges remain. The complexity of clan dynamics, the prevalence of armed groups, and external interference pose significant obstacles to the reconciliation process. However, the resilience and determination of the Somali people, coupled with continued support from the international community, hold the promise of a brighter future for Somalia.

In conclusion, national reconciliation efforts are a vital component of Somalia's journey towards peace and stability. By fostering dialogue, addressing grievances, and promoting social cohesion, these initiatives contribute to a more inclusive and resilient society. While challenges persist, the commitment of both Somali stakeholders and international actors underscores the importance of national reconciliation in building a peaceful and prosperous Somalia.

Challenges to State-Building: Corruption and Security

In the subchapter "Challenges to State-Building: Corruption and Security" of the book "Somalia: A Painful History of Struggle and Resilience," we delve into two critical obstacles that have hindered the progress of Somalia's state-building efforts – corruption and security concerns. This chapter aims to provide diplomats, educators, teachers, journalists, politicians, and legislators, as well as individuals interested in the niches of Somali history, politics, culture, and socio-economic development, with a comprehensive understanding of the impact and implications of corruption and security challenges on Somalia's state-building process.

Corruption has plagued Somalia for decades, hindering the establishment of a strong, accountable, and transparent government. The absence of effective governance structures, weak legal frameworks, and a culture of impunity have allowed corruption to thrive. This subchapter examines the pervasive nature of corruption in Somalia, exploring its causes, manifestations, and consequences. It sheds light on how corruption erodes public trust, undermines institutional capacity, diverts public resources, and perpetuates social inequalities, ultimately impeding the state-building process.

Moreover, the subchapter delves into the complex security challenges facing Somalia. The country has been grappling with protracted conflicts, terrorism, and the presence of armed groups, which have severely undermined stability and hindered state-building efforts. We explore the origins and various actors involved in the conflict, including the rise of extremist groups such as Al-Shabaab. Additionally, the subchapter examines the impact of security challenges on the lives of ordinary Somalis, the displacement of populations, and the consequences for regional stability.

By highlighting the intertwined issues of corruption and security, this subchapter underscores the need for a holistic approach to state-building in Somalia. It explores potential strategies and solutions, such as strengthening governance structures, fostering accountability, promoting transparency, and enhancing security cooperation at the national and international levels.

Overall, this subchapter aims to provide a comprehensive analysis of the challenges posed by corruption and security concerns to Somalia's state-building process. It serves as a valuable resource for diplomats, educators, teachers, journalists, politicians, and legislators, as well as individuals interested in understanding the complexities of Somalia's history, politics, culture, and socio-economic development.

Chapter 4: Somali Piracy: Origins, Trends, and International Response

Factors Contributing to the Rise of Somali Piracy

Piracy off the coast of Somalia has been a pressing issue for international security and maritime trade in recent years. This subchapter aims to analyze the factors that have contributed to the rise of Somali piracy, providing a comprehensive understanding of the origins and trends of this phenomenon.

The first contributing factor to the rise of Somali piracy is the political instability in the country. Following the collapse of the Somali government in 1991, a power vacuum was created, allowing criminal networks to thrive. With no functioning authority to enforce law and order, piracy became an attractive and lucrative alternative for many young men in the coastal communities.

Additionally, poverty and economic challenges have played a significant role in fostering the growth of piracy. Lack of employment opportunities and limited access to basic services have pushed individuals towards piracy as a means of survival. Unemployment rates in Somalia remain high, especially among the youth, making piracy an appealing option for financial gain.

Moreover, the absence of effective governance and law enforcement has allowed piracy to flourish. The weak legal framework and corruption within the Somali judicial system have created an environment conducive to piracy activities. This has made it difficult for international navies and law enforcement agencies to effectively combat piracy in the region.

Another factor contributing to the rise of piracy is the availability of weapons. The Somali civil war and its aftermath have left the country awash with arms, making it easier for pirates to carry out their operations. The easy accessibility to weapons has increased the sophistication and violence of pirate attacks, posing a significant threat to maritime security.

Lastly, the lack of a strong international response has also contributed to the rise of Somali piracy. Until recently, there was a lack of coordinated efforts by the international community to address the root causes of piracy and provide assistance to Somalia. This has allowed piracy to persist and evolve over the years, requiring a more comprehensive and integrated approach from the international community.

In conclusion, a combination of political instability, poverty, weak governance, availability of weapons, and a lack of international response has contributed to the rise of Somali piracy. To effectively combat piracy, it is crucial to address these underlying factors and work towards establishing stability, economic development, and effective governance in Somalia.

Poverty, Unemployment, and Economic Motivations

In the complex tapestry of Somalia's history, poverty, unemployment, and economic motivations have played a significant role in shaping the country's trajectory. These interconnected issues have had profound implications for the Somali people and have reverberated throughout the region. Understanding their causes, consequences, and potential solutions is crucial for diplomats, educators, teachers, journalists, politicians, and legislators seeking to engage with Somalia's challenges and opportunities.

The origins of poverty in Somalia can be traced back to a combination of factors, including colonial exploitation, civil war, and political instability. These factors have hindered the development of a robust and diversified economy, leaving many Somalis trapped in a cycle of poverty. The lack of access to basic services, such as education and healthcare, exacerbates the challenges faced by the population.

Unemployment is another pressing issue in Somalia, particularly among the youth. With limited job opportunities and a growing population, the lack of employment prospects has fueled social unrest and contributed to the rise of extremist groups. Addressing unemployment requires not only creating jobs but also investing in vocational training and entrepreneurship programs that can empower Somalis to build their own livelihoods.

Economic motivations, on the other hand, have driven both positive and negative dynamics in Somalia. On one hand, economic aspirations have led to the growth of the Somali diaspora, with many Somalis seeking better opportunities abroad. The diaspora has made significant contributions to the countries they have settled in, as well as to Somalia itself through remittances and investments.

However, economic motivations have also fueled piracy, a phenomenon that emerged in response to illegal fishing and toxic waste dumping off the Somali coast. The international community has responded to piracy by deploying naval forces and implementing strategies to deter and combat piracy. Nevertheless, addressing the root causes of piracy requires addressing poverty, unemployment, and the lack of economic opportunities that make piracy an attractive option for some.

To overcome the challenges posed by poverty, unemployment, and economic motivations, Somalia requires a multifaceted approach. This approach should include investment in infrastructure, education, and healthcare to create an enabling environment for economic growth. Additionally, fostering entrepreneurship and promoting job creation can empower the Somali people to build sustainable livelihoods.

Efforts to tackle poverty and unemployment should also be complemented by initiatives to address social inequalities and promote inclusive economic growth. Empowering women and marginalized groups is crucial for achieving sustainable development and reducing poverty.

By understanding the complex interplay between poverty, unemployment, and economic motivations, diplomats, educators, teachers, journalists, politicians, and legislators can contribute to the formulation of informed policies and strategies that can help Somalia overcome these challenges and seize the opportunities for development.

Weak Maritime Security and Law Enforcement

Somalia's maritime security and law enforcement have long been a cause for concern, both domestically and internationally. This subchapter aims to shed light on the challenges and consequences of weak maritime security and law enforcement in Somalia, addressing a wide range of audiences including diplomats, educators, teachers, journalists, politicians, and legislators.

The Somali waters have been plagued by various security threats, including piracy, illegal fishing, and smuggling. These activities have not only hindered Somalia's economic growth but also posed a significant risk to international trade and security. Piracy, in particular, has gained global attention due to its impact on maritime commerce and the safety of seafarers. This subchapter explores the origins and trends of Somali piracy and delves into the international response to combat this menace.

Furthermore, this subchapter examines the root causes of weak maritime security and law enforcement in Somalia. It traces the origins of political instability in the country and its impact on the ability to maintain effective control over coastal areas. The influence of clan dynamics on politics and society is also analyzed to provide a comprehensive understanding of the challenges faced in establishing a robust maritime security framework.

In addition to the challenges, opportunities for development and improvement in Somalia's maritime security and law enforcement are explored. The subchapter discusses the potential for international collaboration, capacity-building initiatives, and investment in infrastructure to enhance Somalia's ability to combat maritime threats effectively.

This subchapter is an essential read for those interested in understanding the historical context, current challenges, and potential solutions regarding weak maritime security and law enforcement in Somalia. It provides valuable insights for diplomats seeking to engage with Somalia, educators and teachers aiming to educate their students about Somalia's struggles, journalists covering maritime security issues, politicians and legislators involved in crafting policies, and concerned individuals who wish to contribute to the improvement of Somalia's maritime security and law enforcement.

Overall, this subchapter highlights the urgency of addressing weak maritime security and law enforcement and emphasizes the need for a comprehensive and collaborative approach to tackle these challenges effectively.

Evolution of Somali Piracy: Tactics and Trends

Since the early 2000s, the world has witnessed the rise of Somali piracy, a phenomenon that has posed significant challenges to global maritime security. This subchapter explores the evolution of Somali piracy, examining the tactics employed by pirates and the trends that have emerged over the years.

Somali piracy initially emerged as a response to the deteriorating economic and political conditions in Somalia. With the collapse of the central government in 1991 and the ensuing civil war, Somalia's once-thriving fishing industry was severely affected. Disgruntled fishermen turned to piracy as a means of survival, hijacking vessels and demanding hefty ransoms.

In the early stages, Somali pirates relied on simple tactics, such as armed boarding and the use of small skiffs to approach and board ships. However, as international naval forces increased their presence in the region, pirates adapted their tactics to evade capture. They began using larger mother ships to extend their range and employed more sophisticated weaponry, including rocket-propelled grenades and automatic rifles.

Moreover, pirates started employing tactics such as violence, intimidation, and hostage-taking to exert control over their targets. This shift in tactics led to an increase in violence against crew members, maritime security personnel, and hostages, further alarming the international community.

Over time, trends in Somali piracy have evolved as a response to international counter-piracy efforts. Naval patrols and increased security measures on merchant vessels have forced pirates to become more inventive. They have resorted to tactics such as hijacking fishing trawlers and using them as bases of operation, as well as employing ransom-negotiating intermediaries to distance themselves from direct negotiations.

Furthermore, Somali pirates have expanded their operational range, venturing into the Indian Ocean and even attempting hijackings as far as the Seychelles. This expansion demonstrates the adaptability and resilience of Somali pirates in the face of international efforts to curtail their activities.

The international response to Somali piracy has been multifaceted, involving naval patrols, legal frameworks, and collaborations with regional states. However, the issue remains complex, and a comprehensive solution has yet to be found.

In conclusion, the evolution of Somali piracy has seen pirates adapt their tactics and employ more sophisticated methods in response to international counter-piracy efforts. This subchapter aims to provide diplomats, educators, journalists, and politicians with an understanding of the changing dynamics of Somali piracy, enabling them to develop more effective strategies to combat this threat to maritime security.

Hijackings, Ransom Negotiations, and Crew Safety

The issue of hijackings, ransom negotiations, and crew safety has plagued Somalia for decades, contributing to the country's painful history of struggle and resilience. This subchapter aims to shed light on the complexities surrounding these incidents and their far-reaching implications.

Somalia's strategic location along the Horn of Africa has made it vulnerable to piracy and hijackings, particularly in the waters of the Gulf of Aden and the Indian Ocean. The rise of piracy in the early 2000s was a direct consequence of the country's political instability, weak governance, and economic desperation. As warlords and armed groups took control of various regions, they turned to piracy as a means to generate income and exert influence.

The international response to Somali piracy has been multifaceted, involving naval patrols, private security firms, and ransom negotiations. Diplomatic efforts have aimed to address the root causes of piracy, such as poverty and governance issues, while also focusing on suppressing piracy activities through coordinated military operations. However, finding a lasting solution has proven challenging due to the complex nature of the problem.

Ransom negotiations have been a controversial aspect of dealing with piracy. While paying ransoms has often been the quickest way to secure the release of hijacked vessels and crew members, it also perpetuates the cycle of piracy by providing financial incentives for pirates to continue their operations. This dilemma has forced governments, shipping companies, and international organizations to grapple with ethical questions and seek alternative strategies to protect crew members and vessels.

Crew safety remains a paramount concern in the face of hijackings and piracy. The physical and psychological toll on seafarers subjected to prolonged captivity is significant. Efforts to enhance crew safety have included the deployment of armed guards on vessels, improved security protocols, and the establishment of regional training centers to equip seafarers with the necessary skills to navigate dangerous waters.

As diplomats, educators, teachers, journalists, politicians, and legislators, understanding the dynamics of hijackings, ransom negotiations, and crew safety is crucial in developing effective policies and strategies to combat piracy and protect vulnerable populations. By addressing the root causes of piracy, strengthening governance structures, and promoting economic development, we can contribute to Somalia's journey towards stability and resilience.

International Naval Operations and Counter-Piracy Measures

In recent years, the issue of piracy off the coast of Somalia has garnered significant global attention. As ships carrying valuable cargo traversed the waters, armed pirates took advantage of the country's political instability and lack of effective governance to seize vessels and hold crew members hostage for ransom. This subchapter explores the international naval operations and counter-piracy measures that have been implemented to combat this menace.

Naval operations conducted by various countries, such as the United States, European Union, and regional partners like India and China, have played a crucial role in deterring and suppressing piracy in the region. These operations involve the deployment of warships, aircraft, and surveillance technology to monitor the waters, patrol key shipping routes, and respond to distress calls. The presence of these naval forces has not only disrupted pirate activities but also provided protection to merchant vessels, ensuring the safe passage of goods and safeguarding the lives of seafarers.

Furthermore, international collaboration has been instrumental in addressing this transnational problem. The Contact Group on Piracy off the Coast of Somalia, comprising more than 80 nations and organizations, has facilitated coordination and information sharing among member states. This collective effort has led to the establishment of multinational naval task forces, such as Combined Task Force 151, which have been highly effective in reducing piracy incidents.

Counter-piracy measures extend beyond military operations. Efforts to address the root causes of piracy have focused on capacity building, governance reforms, and economic development in Somalia. International assistance has supported initiatives to strengthen the country's maritime law enforcement capabilities, enhance the rule of law, and promote economic opportunities for coastal communities. Additionally, initiatives to combat piracy have incorporated legal frameworks for prosecuting pirates, as well as efforts to disrupt their financing and dismantle their networks.

The success of international naval operations and counter-piracy measures should not be understated. Piracy incidents off the coast of Somalia have significantly declined in recent years, and the protection provided to maritime trade has contributed to regional stability and economic development. However, challenges remain, including the need for sustained international support, continued capacity building efforts, and addressing the underlying socio-economic factors that drive individuals to engage in piracy.

In conclusion, international naval operations and counter-piracy measures have played a vital role in combating piracy off the coast of Somalia. Through collaborative efforts, naval forces have disrupted pirate activities, protected merchant vessels, and contributed to regional stability. However, addressing the root causes of piracy and ensuring long-term success require sustained international support and a comprehensive approach that encompasses governance reforms and economic development in Somalia.

Addressing the Issue: International Cooperation and Long-term Solutions

In a world that is increasingly interconnected, the issue of international cooperation has become paramount in addressing the many challenges faced by countries around the globe. This is particularly true for Somalia, a country that has endured a painful history of struggle and resilience. In order to overcome the numerous obstacles it faces, Somalia must seek long-term solutions through international cooperation.

For diplomats, educators, teachers, journalists, politicians, and legislators, understanding the importance of international cooperation in addressing Somalia's challenges is crucial. The key to finding lasting solutions lies in collaboration, dialogue, and the sharing of knowledge and expertise. By working together, we can pool resources and find innovative approaches to tackle the complex issues that Somalia faces.

One of the core issues that requires international cooperation is the history of Somalia's civil war and its consequences. This chapter will explore the causes and consequences of the civil war, shedding light on the deep-rooted divisions and grievances that have fueled the conflict. By understanding the underlying causes, we can begin to develop strategies that promote reconciliation and peacebuilding.

Political instability is another pressing concern in Somalia, and its origins and impact need to be addressed through international cooperation. By examining the historical context and the dynamics of Somali politics, we can identify ways to support the development of stable and accountable governance structures.

Somalia's struggle with piracy is yet another area where international cooperation is crucial. By exploring the origins and trends of piracy in the region, we can understand the underlying socio-economic factors that contribute to this phenomenon. Through coordinated efforts, we can develop comprehensive strategies that address the root causes of piracy and provide alternative livelihoods for local communities.

Additionally, international cooperation is vital in supporting the political struggle for independence in Somaliland. By recognizing the unique aspirations of the people of Somaliland and engaging in dialogue, we can contribute to a peaceful resolution that respects the self-determination of its inhabitants.

The Somali diaspora also plays a significant role in the country's development, and their cultural identity and contributions deserve recognition. By fostering connections and engaging with the Somali diaspora, we can tap into their skills, resources, and expertise to support Somalia's progress.

As we delve into the complexities of Somali society, it is essential to understand the influence of clan dynamics on politics and society. By examining the historical context and power dynamics within clans, we can work towards creating inclusive political systems that give voice to all Somali citizens.

Somali refugees face unique challenges in the global context, and international cooperation is crucial in providing them with the support they need to rebuild their lives. By addressing their specific needs and promoting their resilience, we can ensure their successful integration into host communities.

Efforts towards empowering Somali women and achieving gender equality also require international cooperation. By supporting initiatives that promote women's rights, education, and economic empowerment, we can create a more inclusive and equitable society.

Finally, international cooperation plays a vital role in preserving Somali art, literature, and cultural expressions amidst conflict. By supporting artists and providing platforms for cultural exchange, we can help foster a sense of national identity and pride.

Ultimately, international cooperation is essential in addressing the challenges faced by Somalia. By bringing together diplomats, educators, teachers, journalists, politicians, and legislators, we can develop long-term solutions that promote peace, stability, and development in this resilient nation.

Legal Frameworks and Prosecution of Pirates

Piracy has long plagued the waters off the coast of Somalia, causing economic disruptions, endangering international trade, and threatening the safety and security of maritime activities. This subchapter will explore the legal frameworks and prosecution methods employed to combat this menace, with a particular focus on the international response and the role of Somalia's legal system.

The international community, recognizing the urgency and gravity of the piracy problem, has taken significant steps to address it. The United Nations Security Council, through various resolutions, has called upon states to cooperate in the fight against piracy and has authorized the use of force to suppress acts of piracy in the region. These resolutions have provided a legal basis for naval operations, such as the European Union's Operation Atalanta and the United States-led Combined Task Force 151, to patrol the waters off the coast of Somalia and apprehend pirates.

Additionally, the international community has developed legal frameworks to facilitate the prosecution of pirates. The United Nations Convention on the Law of the Sea (UNCLOS) establishes the legal framework for combating piracy, defining piracy as a crime under international law and outlining the jurisdiction and legal obligations of states. Moreover, the International Maritime Organization (IMO) has developed guidance and best practices for states to follow in investigating and prosecuting pirates.

Within Somalia itself, efforts have been made to strengthen the legal system and enhance the capacity to prosecute pirates. The Somali government, with the support of international partners, has established specialized courts and prisons to handle piracy cases. These courts, known as the Somali High Court Specialized Division for Maritime Offenses, have been instrumental in prosecuting and convicting pirates, sending a strong message that piracy will not be tolerated.

However, challenges remain in effectively prosecuting pirates. The lack of capacity and resources, corruption, and the sheer magnitude of the problem pose significant obstacles. There is a need for continued international support, both in terms of financial resources and technical assistance, to strengthen Somalia's legal system and ensure the successful prosecution of pirates.

In conclusion, the international community has implemented legal frameworks and prosecution methods to combat piracy off the coast of Somalia. The United Nations, through resolutions and conventions, has provided a legal basis for naval operations and established guidelines for states to follow. Within Somalia, specialized courts have been established to prosecute pirates, but challenges persist. Continued international support is crucial to strengthen Somalia's legal system and effectively combat piracy in the region.

Maritime Development and Economic Opportunities

The maritime sector plays a vital role in the development and economic opportunities of Somalia, a country with over 3,300 kilometers of coastline. The potential for growth and prosperity in this sector is immense, and it is essential for diplomats, educators, teachers, journalists, politicians, legislators, and other stakeholders to understand the significance of maritime development in Somalia's history of struggle and resilience.

Historically, Somalia has been a crucial hub for trade and commerce, connecting Africa, Asia, and the Middle East. Its strategic location along major shipping routes has made it a gateway for international trade. However, decades of conflict and political instability have hindered the country's ability to capitalize on its maritime resources fully.

The restoration of stability in Somalia has opened up new opportunities for maritime development. The Somali government, in collaboration with international partners, has taken steps to revive the country's maritime sector. Efforts have been made to improve port infrastructure, enhance maritime security, and strengthen maritime governance. These initiatives are aimed at attracting foreign investment, boosting trade, and creating employment opportunities for the Somali people.

Investment in maritime infrastructure is crucial for Somalia's economic growth. The development of modern ports and terminals will facilitate the efficient movement of goods and promote regional and international trade. Improved connectivity will not only benefit

Somalia but also its neighboring countries, fostering economic integration and cooperation.

The fight against piracy in Somali waters has also been a priority for the international community. Through coordinated efforts, piracy incidents have significantly decreased in recent years. This positive trend has restored confidence in the region's maritime security and has encouraged more vessels to utilize Somali waters, further promoting economic activities.

Somalia's potential for offshore oil and gas exploration is another area of interest for economic development. The country's vast maritime territory holds significant untapped resources, and exploration efforts are underway. The successful exploitation of these resources could provide a substantial boost to Somalia's economy and contribute to its long-term stability.

Furthermore, the maritime sector offers numerous opportunities for job creation and skills development. Investing in maritime education and training programs will equip Somali youth with the necessary skills to participate in the industry. This, in turn, will contribute to poverty reduction and social development, empowering the Somali people and promoting a sustainable future.

In conclusion, maritime development presents immense economic opportunities for Somalia. By investing in port infrastructure, enhancing maritime security, and exploring offshore resources, the country can unlock its full potential and reclaim its historical position as a center of trade and commerce. It is crucial for diplomats, educators, teachers, journalists, politicians, legislators, and other stakeholders to recognize the importance of maritime development and support initiatives that promote economic growth and stability in Somalia.

Chapter 5: Somaliland: Political Struggle for Independence

Historical Background: Somaliland's Quest for Sovereignty

Somaliland, a self-declared independent state in the Horn of Africa, has a rich historical background that has shaped its quest for sovereignty. This subchapter explores the historical factors that have contributed to Somaliland's political struggle for independence.

The story of Somaliland's quest for sovereignty begins with the colonial era. In the late 19th century, the region was colonized by European powers, with Britain taking control of the northern part, known as British Somaliland. Under British rule, the region experienced relative stability and development, which laid the foundation for its future aspirations.

However, the story took a different turn in 1960 when British Somaliland gained independence and subsequently united with Italian Somaliland to form the Somali Republic. This union, though initially seen as a promise of unity and prosperity, soon turned sour. The central government in Mogadishu marginalized and suppressed the aspirations of the people of Somaliland, leading to growing discontent and a sense of political and economic marginalization.

The turning point came in 1991 when the collapse of the Somali Republic plunged the country into a devastating civil war. In the chaos that followed, Somaliland declared its independence from Somalia and sought to establish its own government and institutions. Despite facing numerous challenges, including lack of international recognition, Somaliland managed to establish a functioning state with a constitution, a democratically elected government, and a legal system.

The historical background of Somaliland's quest for sovereignty is crucial for diplomats, educators, journalists, and politicians to understand. It sheds light on the complex dynamics of the Somali conflict and the aspirations of the people of Somaliland. It also offers insights into the challenges and opportunities that arise from the pursuit of self-determination and independence.

For educators and teachers, understanding the historical background of Somaliland's quest for sovereignty provides a valuable perspective when teaching about the Somali Civil War, political instability, and clan dynamics in Somalia. It helps students grasp the complexities of the conflict and encourages critical thinking about the political struggles faced by marginalized communities.

Journalists and politicians can benefit from this historical background to provide accurate and nuanced reporting on the political situation in the region. It helps them contextualize current events and avoid simplistic narratives that overlook the historical factors at play.

In conclusion, the historical background of Somaliland's quest for sovereignty is a crucial chapter in the book "Somalia: A Painful History of Struggle and Resilience." It is relevant to diplomats, educators, teachers, journalists, politicians, and legislators interested in understanding the Somali conflict and its various dimensions. By exploring this history, we can gain a deeper appreciation for the challenges and aspirations of the people of Somaliland as they continue to strive for recognition and self-determination.

British Protectorate and Independence

The subchapter "British Protectorate and Independence" delves into a critical period in Somalia's history, exploring the impact of British colonial rule and the eventual struggle for independence. This chapter provides valuable insights for diplomats, educators, teachers, journalists, politicians, and legislators, as well as those interested in understanding the origins of Somalia's complex political and social dynamics.

During the late 19th century, European powers were vying for control over Africa, and Somalia became a battleground for colonial interests. In 1884, Britain established a protectorate in the northern regions of Somalia, known as British Somaliland, primarily as a strategic outpost for its imperial ambitions. This marked the beginning of a tumultuous relationship between the Somali people and the British colonial administration.

Under British rule, the region experienced some infrastructural development, including the establishment of schools and hospitals. However, this period was also marked by economic exploitation and political marginalization, as the British authorities prioritized their own interests over those of the Somali people. This sparked a growing sense of nationalism and resistance, laying the foundation for the eventual struggle for independence.

The subchapter explores the emergence of political movements and leaders who spearheaded the fight for self-determination. Figures like Mohamed Abdullah Hassan, known as the "Mad Mullah," and the Somali Youth League (SYL) played crucial roles in mobilizing the Somali population against British rule. Their efforts culminated in the attainment of independence on July 1, 1960, when the former British Somaliland and the Italian-administered Trust Territory of Somalia merged to form the Somali Republic.

However, the journey towards independence did not bring stability to Somalia. The chapter also delves into the challenges that arose during the post-independence era, such as tribal rivalries, political instability, and the failure to establish effective governance structures. These factors would contribute to the eventual outbreak of the Somali Civil War in 1991, which had profound consequences for the country and its people.

By examining the British Protectorate era and the subsequent struggle for independence, this subchapter provides a comprehensive understanding of Somalia's historical trajectory. It sheds light on the complex factors that have shaped the country's political, social, and economic landscape, allowing diplomats, educators, teachers, journalists, politicians, and legislators to gain a more nuanced perspective on Somalia's past and its ongoing struggles and resilience.

Somaliland's Unrecognized Status

In the vast landscape of Somalia's painful history, the subchapter titled "Somaliland's Unrecognized Status" aims to shed light on the political struggle for independence faced by the self-declared Republic of Somaliland. This section is specifically addressed to diplomats, educators, teachers, journalists, politicians, and legislators who seek a comprehensive understanding of Somalia's complex dynamics. It also caters to the niches of Somali history, political instability, Somali diaspora, and Somali economy, among others.

Somaliland, a region located in the northwestern part of Somalia, declared its independence from the central government in 1991 following the collapse of the Somali state. Since then, it has sought international recognition as a separate entity, but its efforts have been met with significant challenges. Despite establishing a functioning government, maintaining relative stability, and conducting free and fair elections, Somaliland remains unrecognized by the international community.

The subchapter explores the origins and consequences of Somaliland's unrecognized status. It delves into the factors that have contributed to its political struggle for independence, including historical grievances, clan dynamics, and the impact of the Somali civil war. By examining the origins of Somaliland's quest for self-determination, readers gain a deeper understanding of the region's unique circumstances and the motivations behind its desire for recognition.

Furthermore, this section explores the impact of Somaliland's unrecognized status on its people, economy, and development prospects. It highlights the challenges faced by the region, such as limited access to international aid, trade barriers, and hindered foreign direct investment. Additionally, it delves into the opportunities that recognition could bring, including increased economic development, diplomatic engagement, and access to global institutions.

The subchapter also analyzes the international response to Somaliland's bid for recognition. It looks at the role of regional organizations, neighboring countries, and international actors in shaping the discourse surrounding Somaliland's status. By examining the reasons behind the lack of recognition, readers gain insights into the complexities and interests that influence international politics.

Overall, "Somaliland's Unrecognized Status" provides a comprehensive examination of the political struggle faced by Somaliland in its pursuit of international recognition. It presents a nuanced understanding of the region's historical background, political dynamics, and socio-economic challenges, aiming to inform and engage diplomats, educators, teachers, journalists, politicians, and legislators in a meaningful discussion about Somalia's complex reality.

Governance and Stability in Somaliland

Somaliland, a self-declared independent state in the Horn of Africa, stands out as a beacon of governance and stability amidst the tumultuous history of Somalia. This subchapter explores the unique political landscape and the commendable efforts made by the people and leaders of Somaliland in achieving stability, fostering good governance, and promoting development.

Since declaring independence in 1991, Somaliland has strived to establish effective governance structures and institutions. The political system is based on a multi-party democracy, with regular elections held at various levels. The democratic process has been embraced by both the government and the citizens, leading to peaceful transitions of power and ensuring the stability of the state.

One of the key factors contributing to governance and stability in Somaliland is the commitment to the rule of law. The judiciary system is independent and has successfully resolved disputes, ensuring that justice is served. Additionally, the government has implemented legal reforms to protect human rights, promote gender equality, and enhance the overall well-being of its citizens.

Education is another cornerstone of governance in Somaliland. The government has invested heavily in the education sector, providing access to quality education for all its citizens. This commitment to education has not only empowered the population but has also laid the foundation for a knowledgeable and skilled workforce, driving economic growth and development.

In terms of economic governance, Somaliland has made notable strides. The government has implemented policies that encourage foreign investment, promote entrepreneurship, and foster economic diversification. This has resulted in increased job opportunities, improved living standards, and reduced poverty rates.

The stability and governance achieved in Somaliland have not gone unnoticed by the international community. Diplomats, educators, journalists, and policymakers from around the world have recognized Somaliland's achievements and have engaged with its leaders to learn from their experiences. The lessons learned from Somaliland's success story can serve as a source of inspiration for other countries facing similar challenges.

In conclusion, the governance and stability achieved in Somaliland are a testament to the resilience and determination of its people. Through a commitment to democracy, the rule of law, education, and economic development, Somaliland has been able to overcome the challenges it faced and create a prosperous and stable state. The experiences of Somaliland offer valuable insights for diplomats, educators, journalists, politicians, and legislators, as well as those interested in the history, politics, and development of Somalia and its diaspora.

Political Institutions and Democratization

In the complex landscape of Somali history, understanding the role of political institutions and their impact on the process of democratization is crucial. This subchapter aims to shed light on the challenges, progress, and potential solutions in fostering democratic governance in Somalia, a country that has experienced significant political instability and civil strife.

Political institutions play a pivotal role in shaping the trajectory of democratization. They provide the framework within which political processes, such as elections, governance, and decision-making, take place. In Somalia, a country plagued by years of conflict and instability, the establishment of effective political institutions has been a formidable task. However, recent efforts have shown promising signs of progress.

The Somali Civil War, with its complex causes and far-reaching consequences, has deeply affected the political landscape of the country. It shattered existing political institutions and created a power vacuum, leading to a prolonged period of instability. This chapter will explore the causes and consequences of the civil war, examining how it has shaped the political trajectory of Somalia.

Political instability in Somalia has its origins in a multitude of factors, including clan dynamics, foreign intervention, and weak governance structures. Understanding these origins is crucial for developing effective strategies to address political instability and foster democratization. This chapter will delve into the historical context that has led to the current state of affairs and examine the impact of political instability on the country's development.

Somali piracy, a phenomenon that gained international attention in recent years, is another manifestation of political instability and state fragility. This subchapter will explore the origins and trends of Somali piracy, as well as the international response to this maritime security threat.

The struggle for independence in Somaliland, a self-declared state within Somalia, highlights the complexities of political dynamics in the region. This chapter will examine the political struggle for recognition and the implications it has for the broader process of democratization in Somalia.

The Somali diaspora, with its cultural identity and contributions, also plays a significant role in shaping the political landscape of the country. This subchapter will explore the influence of the diaspora on political processes and their potential contributions to democratization efforts.

Clan dynamics have long influenced politics and society in Somalia. This chapter will delve into the intricate web of clan relationships and how they impact political institutions and democratization processes.

Despite immense challenges, Somali refugees have shown remarkable resilience in the face of adversity. This subchapter will examine the challenges faced by Somali refugees and how their experiences can inform broader discussions on global refugee issues.

Efforts to empower Somali women and promote gender equality are crucial for the democratization process. This chapter will explore the initiatives undertaken to empower women and the progress made in achieving gender equality in Somalia.

Somali art and literature serve as important expressions of cultural identity amidst conflict. This subchapter will explore the role of art and literature in preserving and promoting Somali culture, as well as their potential to contribute to peacebuilding and democratization.

Finally, the Somali economy presents both challenges and opportunities for development. This chapter will analyze the economic challenges faced by the country and explore potential avenues for sustainable economic growth and development.

In conclusion, this subchapter on political institutions and democratization in Somalia provides an in-depth analysis of the challenges, progress, and potential solutions in fostering democratic governance. It is essential reading for diplomats, educators, teachers, journalists, politicians, and legislators interested in understanding the complex political dynamics of Somalia and its path towards democratization.

Economic Development and Foreign Relations

In the complex socio-political landscape of Somalia, economic development and foreign relations have played a crucial role in shaping the country's trajectory. This subchapter delves into the challenges and opportunities that Somalia has faced in its pursuit of economic growth and the impact of foreign relations on its development.

As Somalia emerged from the ashes of decades-long conflict, the need for economic revitalization became apparent. However, achieving economic stability has been an uphill battle due to various factors such as political instability, weak institutions, and a lack of infrastructure. The chapter explores these challenges in detail, shedding light on their origins and their impact on the country's economic growth.

Foreign relations have also played a significant role in Somalia's economic development. The chapter examines the nation's engagement with the international community, focusing on the assistance received from foreign governments, international organizations, and non-governmental organizations. It explores the impact of these relationships on Somalia's economic progress and the opportunities they have presented for development.

For diplomats and politicians, this subchapter provides insights into the importance of foreign relations in supporting Somalia's economic growth. It highlights the need for continued international collaboration and assistance to overcome the challenges faced by the country.

Educators and teachers will find this subchapter valuable in understanding the complexities of Somalia's economic development. It equips them with the knowledge needed to educate students about the challenges and opportunities that Somalia has faced in its pursuit of economic stability.

Journalists will find this subchapter useful in their coverage of Somalia's economic landscape. It provides a comprehensive overview of the factors influencing economic development and the impact of foreign relations, enabling journalists to report on these issues accurately and effectively.

Furthermore, legislators will gain insights into the importance of policies that promote economic development and foster positive foreign relations. The subchapter highlights the role of legislation in creating an enabling environment for economic growth and attracting foreign investment.

Overall, this subchapter serves as a valuable resource for diplomats, educators, teachers, journalists, politicians, and legislators interested in understanding the intricacies of Somalia's economic development and its relationship with foreign relations. By examining the challenges faced and the opportunities available, it provides a comprehensive perspective on Somalia's journey towards economic stability and growth.

International Recognition: Challenges and Prospects

In the book "Somalia: A Painful History of Struggle and Resilience," the subchapter on "International Recognition: Challenges and Prospects" delves into the complexities of Somalia's relationship with the global community. Addressing a diverse audience of diplomats, educators, teachers, journalists, politicians, and legislators, this subchapter aims to shed light on the challenges Somalia faces in gaining international recognition and the prospects for a brighter future.

For decades, Somalia has struggled to establish itself as a recognized and respected nation on the global stage. The country has been marred by political instability, civil war, piracy, and economic challenges. These issues have hindered Somalia's ability to gain the international recognition it seeks and deserves.

One of the main challenges Somalia faces in obtaining international recognition is the perception of political instability. The origins and impact of this instability are explored in earlier chapters of the book, highlighting the need for a stable and functioning government that can effectively engage with the international community. The subchapter emphasizes the importance of international support in helping Somalia overcome these challenges and build a strong foundation for political stability.

Another obstacle to international recognition is the issue of Somali piracy. The subchapter delves into the origins, trends, and international response to piracy off the coast of Somalia, highlighting the collaborative efforts required to combat this menace. By addressing piracy, Somalia can enhance its credibility and demonstrate its commitment to maintaining maritime security.

Prospects for international recognition lie in the political struggle for independence in Somaliland, a self-declared state within Somalia. The subchapter explores the dynamics of this struggle and its potential impact on Somalia's international standing. By examining the political aspirations of Somaliland, the book aims to provoke thought and discussion among the audience, encouraging them to consider the complexities of recognizing a breakaway region within a fragile state.

Recognizing the contributions of the Somali diaspora is also crucial in gaining international recognition. The subchapter highlights the cultural identity and significant contributions of Somalis living abroad, showcasing their potential to bridge the gap between Somalia and the international community.

In conclusion, the subchapter on "International Recognition: Challenges and Prospects" delves into the complexities of Somalia's relationship with the global community. It addresses the challenges posed by political instability, piracy, and the struggle for independence in Somaliland. By exploring these issues and highlighting the potential for a brighter future, the subchapter aims to engage its diverse audience and foster a deeper understanding of the challenges and prospects of Somalia's quest for international recognition.

Diplomatic Efforts and Regional Dynamics

In the subchapter titled "Diplomatic Efforts and Regional Dynamics" of the book "Somalia: A Painful History of Struggle and Resilience," we explore the intricate web of international relations and regional dynamics that have shaped Somalia's past and continue to influence its present.

For decades, Somalia has been plagued by political instability, conflict, and economic challenges. However, diplomatic efforts have played a crucial role in attempting to bring stability and peace to the country. Diplomats, educators, teachers, journalists, politicians, and legislators have all been key stakeholders in these efforts, working tirelessly to find lasting solutions.

One of the significant challenges faced by diplomats in Somalia is navigating the complex web of regional dynamics. Somalia is situated in a region that is itself marred by conflicts, rivalries, and power struggles. The book delves into the historical context of Somalia's relationships with neighboring countries and how these dynamics have influenced the country's political trajectory.

The book also addresses the role of international organizations and initiatives in Somalia. Diplomats from various nations have participated in peace processes, humanitarian aid efforts, and capacity-building programs. These initiatives aim to strengthen governance structures, promote human rights, and support the rebuilding of Somalia's institutions.

Furthermore, the subchapter explores the delicate balance between external intervention and Somali ownership of the peace process. Diplomats and policymakers must consider the aspirations and needs of the Somali people while also addressing regional concerns and interests.

While Somalia has faced numerous challenges, it is essential to acknowledge the progress made through diplomatic efforts. The book highlights successful examples of conflict resolution, peacekeeping, and humanitarian assistance. It also emphasizes the importance of sustained engagement and long-term commitment from the international community.

The subchapter concludes by highlighting the role of diplomats, educators, teachers, journalists, politicians, and legislators in advocating for a comprehensive and inclusive approach to peacebuilding in Somalia. It calls for collaborative efforts that foster dialogue, promote reconciliation, and address the root causes of conflict.

In summary, "Diplomatic Efforts and Regional Dynamics" explores the multifaceted nature of Somalia's diplomatic landscape. It provides insights for diplomats, educators, teachers, journalists, politicians, and legislators into the challenges, achievements, and potential solutions in Somalia's ongoing struggle for stability and resilience.

Implications for Somalia's Unity and Territorial Integrity

The issue of Somalia's unity and territorial integrity has been a subject of great concern and debate, both within the country and among the international community. The ongoing struggles and conflicts in Somalia have had far-reaching implications for its unity as a nation-state and its territorial integrity. This subchapter aims to explore these implications and shed light on the challenges and potential solutions.

Somalia's history of conflict and political instability has had a direct impact on its unity. The collapse of the central government in 1991 led to the emergence of various factions and armed groups vying for power and control. This power vacuum allowed for the rise of separatist movements, such as Somaliland, which declared its independence in 1991. The territorial integrity of Somalia has been further compromised by the autonomy claims of other regions, including Puntland and Jubaland. These divisions have hindered efforts to establish a unified and cohesive government.

The lack of a strong central authority has also created challenges in maintaining Somalia's territorial integrity. The absence of effective governance and security has allowed for the proliferation of armed groups and militias, some of which have engaged in acts of terrorism and piracy. These groups often control and exploit certain regions, further undermining the unity and territorial integrity of the country.

The international community has recognized the importance of Somalia's unity and territorial integrity for regional stability and security. Efforts have been made to support the establishment of a unified and inclusive government through the United Nations and other international organizations. Diplomatic efforts have focused on fostering dialogue and reconciliation among various Somali factions, with the aim of reaching a political settlement that can ensure the country's unity and territorial integrity.

Educators, teachers, and journalists play a crucial role in raising awareness about the implications of Somalia's division and territorial disputes. By providing accurate and objective information, they can contribute to a better understanding of the challenges facing the country and the importance of finding sustainable solutions. Politicians and legislators, both within Somalia and at the international level, have a responsibility to support initiatives that promote unity, reconciliation, and territorial integrity.

In conclusion, the implications for Somalia's unity and territorial integrity are significant and multifaceted. The ongoing conflicts and divisions within the country have hindered efforts to establish a unified government and maintain territorial integrity. However, there is hope for a brighter future through diplomatic efforts, dialogue, and reconciliation. It is important for diplomats, educators, teachers, journalists, politicians, legislators, and all those interested in Somalia's history and future to understand these implications and work towards a peaceful and united Somalia.

Chapter 6: Somali Diaspora: Cultural Identity and Contributions

Diaspora Communities: Historical Context and Global Presence

The Somali diaspora has played a significant role in shaping the history and global presence of the Somali people. From the ancient times of migration to the present day, Somali communities have spread across the globe, establishing themselves in various countries and becoming an integral part of their host societies.

The historical context of Somali diaspora communities can be traced back to ancient times when Somali seafarers and traders ventured far and wide, establishing trade networks and settlements in different parts of the world. These early interactions laid the foundation for the later waves of migration and the formation of diaspora communities.

The global presence of Somali communities today is a testament to their resilience and adaptability. In countries such as the United States, Canada, the United Kingdom, Australia, and Sweden, Somali communities have flourished, contributing to the social, cultural, economic, and political fabric of their host societies. Somali diaspora members have excelled in various fields, including education, business, politics, and the arts, making significant contributions to their respective countries.

For diplomats, educators, teachers, journalists, politicians, and legislators, understanding the historical context and global presence of Somali diaspora communities is crucial. It enables them to appreciate the diversity and richness of Somali culture and identity, as well as the challenges and opportunities faced by diaspora members in their host countries.

The Somali diaspora has also been instrumental in supporting their homeland during times of crisis. When Somalia experienced political instability, civil war, and economic challenges, diaspora communities rallied together to provide humanitarian aid, financial support, and advocacy for peace and stability. Their efforts have been crucial in mitigating the impact of the conflicts and helping Somalia on the path to recovery and development.

Furthermore, the Somali diaspora has served as a bridge between Somalia and the international community. Through their networks and connections, diaspora members have facilitated trade, investment, and cultural exchanges, promoting a better understanding of Somali society and fostering collaboration with other nations.

In conclusion, the historical context and global presence of Somali diaspora communities are of great significance to diplomats, educators, teachers, journalists, politicians, and legislators. Understanding the contributions, challenges, and resilience of Somali diaspora members can help in fostering stronger ties between Somalia and other nations, promoting peace, development, and cultural exchange.

Somali Migration Waves and Diaspora Settlements

Introduction:

One of the defining features of Somalia's history is the widespread migration of its people and the subsequent establishment of diaspora communities around the world. This subchapter explores the various waves of Somali migration and the impact of diaspora settlements on both the host countries and Somalia itself. It delves into the reasons behind these migration waves, the challenges faced by Somali migrants, and the contributions they have made to their host countries and to Somalia's development.

Historical Background:

Somalia has a long history of migration, driven by a variety of factors such as economic opportunities, political instability, and conflicts. The first notable wave of migration occurred during the colonial era when Somalis sought employment in the ports and cities of British and Italian colonies. Subsequent waves followed, including labor migration to the Gulf countries in the 1970s and 1980s, and the flight of refugees during the Somali civil war in the 1990s.

Challenges Faced by Somali Migrants:

Somali migrants have encountered numerous challenges throughout their migration journeys. These include language barriers, cultural adaptation, discrimination, and limited access to education and healthcare. Many have also faced the risk of exploitation and trafficking. Additionally, Somali migrants often grapple with the loss of their cultural identity and the longing for their homeland.

Diaspora Settlements and Contributions:

Despite the challenges, Somali diaspora communities have played a crucial role in the countries they have settled in. They have made significant contributions to the fields of education, healthcare, business, and politics. Somali diaspora entrepreneurs have established successful businesses, creating employment opportunities and stimulating economic growth. In addition, the remittances sent by the diaspora to their families in Somalia have been a lifeline for many during times of crisis.

Impact on Somalia:

The Somali diaspora has not only contributed to their host countries but has also played a vital role in Somalia's development. Many members of the diaspora have returned to Somalia with skills, knowledge, and resources gained abroad, contributing to the reconstruction and development efforts. Furthermore, the diaspora has played a key role in advocating for peace, stability, and good governance in Somalia through various initiatives and organizations.

Conclusion:

The waves of Somali migration and the resulting diaspora settlements have profoundly shaped the history and development of Somalia and its diaspora communities. Understanding the challenges faced by Somali migrants and recognizing their contributions is essential for policymakers, educators, and journalists to effectively engage with the Somali diaspora and support their efforts towards a more prosperous and stable Somalia. Furthermore, fostering stronger ties between Somalia and its diaspora can create opportunities for collaboration and mutual development in various sectors, helping to overcome the country's painful history of struggle and build a resilient and prosperous future.

Cultural Identity and Integration Challenges

In the diverse and complex landscape of Somalia, cultural identity plays a significant role in shaping the country's history, politics, and society. However, the issue of cultural integration has been a persistent challenge, particularly in the face of political instability, clan dynamics, and the impact of the Somali diaspora. This subchapter explores the multifaceted aspects of cultural identity and integration in Somalia, shedding light on the struggles and resilience of the Somali people.

One of the key factors influencing cultural integration in Somalia is the country's painful history of conflict. The Somali Civil War, with its causes and consequences, has deeply affected the social fabric of the nation. As a result, communities have been fragmented, leading to challenges in fostering a sense of national identity. Moreover, political instability and the lack of a stable government have hindered efforts towards cultural integration.

The Somali diaspora, which has spread across the globe, also faces unique challenges in maintaining their cultural identity while adapting to new environments. The Somali diaspora has made significant contributions to their host countries, particularly in areas such as education, business, and the arts. However, they also face the struggle of preserving their cultural heritage and passing it on to future generations amidst the pressure of assimilation.

Clan dynamics, deeply ingrained in Somali society, further complicate the process of cultural integration. Clan affiliations influence political decisions and power dynamics, often overshadowing the development of a collective national identity. Overcoming these challenges requires a delicate balance between acknowledging the importance of clan ties and fostering a cohesive Somali identity.

Despite these obstacles, Somali culture continues to thrive amidst conflict. Somali art, literature, and music serve as powerful forms of cultural expression, providing an outlet for resilience and resistance. Somali women, in particular, have played a significant role in empowering their communities and advocating for gender equality.

The subchapter also explores the challenges faced by Somali refugees in the global context. Forced to flee their homes due to conflict, Somali refugees often struggle to integrate into new societies, facing discrimination and marginalization. However, their resilience and determination to rebuild their lives offer hope for a brighter future.

Finally, the subchapter delves into the economic challenges and opportunities for development in Somalia. Despite the many hurdles, there are pockets of growth and potential for economic progress. By harnessing the country's rich resources and leveraging its strategic location, Somalia can overcome its economic challenges and lay the foundation for a prosperous future.

In conclusion, cultural identity and integration remain significant challenges in Somalia. The country's painful history, political instability, clan dynamics, and the impact of the Somali diaspora all contribute to these challenges. However, by recognizing the importance of cultural expression, empowering Somali women, and fostering a cohesive national identity, Somalia can overcome these obstacles and build a more inclusive and resilient society.

Diaspora Engagement: Remittances and Development
Introduction:
The Somali diaspora, scattered across the globe due to years of conflict and instability, has played a crucial role in the development of their homeland. One of the most significant contributions made by the diaspora is through remittances, which have become a lifeline for many

Somalis. This subchapter explores the impact of diaspora engagement, focusing on remittances and their role in Somalia's development.

Remittances: Economic Lifeline

Remittances are financial transfers made by diaspora members to their families and communities back in Somalia. They have become a vital source of income for many households, contributing to poverty alleviation and economic development. In recent years, Somalia has ranked among the top recipients of remittances in Africa, with estimates suggesting that it receives more than $1.4 billion annually.

Development Impact:

The inflow of remittances has had a transformative effect on various sectors of the Somali economy. It has facilitated investments in education, healthcare, infrastructure, and small businesses, creating employment opportunities and improving living standards. Remittances have also helped minimize the impact of political instability and conflict by providing a safety net for vulnerable populations.

Challenges and Opportunities:

Despite the positive impact, diaspora engagement faces several challenges. High transaction costs, limited financial infrastructure, and regulatory barriers have hindered the full potential of remittances. However, recognizing the importance of remittances, the Somali government has taken steps to address these challenges, including the establishment of specialized remittance companies.

Furthermore, there are opportunities to leverage the diaspora's skills and expertise for broader development. By fostering partnerships between the diaspora and the government, initiatives such as knowledge transfer, capacity building, and investment promotion can be facilitated. This will not only enhance economic development but also contribute to the overall stability and resilience of Somalia.

Conclusion:

Diaspora engagement, particularly through remittances, has emerged as a critical factor in Somalia's development. Remittances have provided a lifeline for many Somalis, enabling them to withstand economic hardships and invest in their communities. However, to fully harness the potential of diaspora engagement, efforts must be made to reduce barriers and create an enabling environment.

For diplomats, educators, teachers, journalists, politicians, and legislators, understanding the significance of diaspora engagement is essential in formulating policies that promote economic development and stability in Somalia. By recognizing the contributions of the diaspora and creating opportunities for their participation, Somalia can continue its journey of resilience and progress.

Economic Contributions and Remittance Flows

In the midst of a turbulent history marked by conflict and instability, Somalia has demonstrated remarkable resilience in its economic endeavors. Despite facing numerous challenges, including a protracted civil war and political instability, the Somali people have shown tremendous resourcefulness and entrepreneurial spirit, making significant contributions to their economy and the global community.

One of the key drivers of Somalia's economy is remittance flows. Remittances, or the money sent by Somalis living abroad to their families and friends back home, play a crucial role in sustaining the country's economy. In fact, Somalia is one of the largest recipients of remittances in the world, with an estimated $1.4 billion flowing into the country annually.

These remittances serve as a lifeline for many Somalis, providing them with much-needed funds for basic necessities such as food, education, and healthcare. Moreover, remittances also serve as an important source of investment capital, fueling entrepreneurial activities and stimulating economic growth. Many small businesses and startups have been launched with the help of remittance funds, creating employment opportunities and contributing to poverty alleviation.

The Somali diaspora, spread across the globe, has played a crucial role in facilitating these remittance flows. Somalis living abroad, particularly in Europe and North America, have established strong networks and remittance transfer systems, ensuring a smooth and efficient flow of funds to their families and communities in Somalia. Furthermore, the Somali diaspora has also made significant contributions to the economies of their adopted countries, excelling in various sectors such as healthcare, education, and entrepreneurship.

Despite the positive impact of remittances, Somalia still faces numerous economic challenges. The lack of a stable financial system, limited access to formal banking services, and a weak regulatory framework pose significant obstacles to economic development. Moreover, the reliance on remittances also exposes the country to external shocks, such as changes in immigration policies or economic downturns in the countries where the diaspora resides.

To overcome these challenges and harness the full potential of their economy, Somalia needs sustained international support and investment. Diplomats, educators, journalists, and politicians must recognize the economic contributions of the Somali people and work towards creating an enabling environment for economic growth. This includes strengthening financial institutions, promoting inclusive economic policies, and fostering entrepreneurship and innovation.

By leveraging the resilience and resourcefulness of its people, Somalia has the potential to transform its economy and become a thriving nation. With the continued support of the international community, Somalia can overcome its painful history and build a prosperous future for its citizens.

Diaspora Organizations and Development Initiatives

The Somali diaspora is a crucial component of the global Somali community, with millions of Somalis living abroad. These individuals and organizations play a significant role in supporting development initiatives in their home country. In this subchapter, we will explore the contributions and impact of diaspora organizations on Somalia's development, addressing an audience of diplomats, educators, teachers, journalists, politicians, and legislators.

Diaspora organizations are instrumental in addressing the challenges faced by Somalia, stemming from its painful history of struggle and resilience. These organizations work tirelessly to bridge the gap between the Somali diaspora and their homeland. They channel resources, expertise, and knowledge to support various development sectors, including education, healthcare, infrastructure, and economic empowerment.

One of the key contributions of diaspora organizations is in the field of education. Recognizing the importance of education in rebuilding a nation, many diaspora-led initiatives focus on improving access to quality education in Somalia. They establish schools, provide scholarships, and enhance teacher training programs, ensuring that Somali youth have the necessary skills to contribute to their country's development.

Healthcare is another sector greatly benefitting from the involvement of diaspora organizations. These organizations support medical facilities, provide medical supplies, and fund training programs for healthcare professionals. By doing so, they strive to improve the healthcare system, which has been severely impacted by years of conflict and instability.

Infrastructure development is also a priority for diaspora organizations. Recognizing the need for improved roads, access to clean water, and reliable electricity, they invest in projects that enhance the country's physical infrastructure. These initiatives not only improve the quality of life for Somalis but also attract foreign investment and create job opportunities.

Furthermore, diaspora organizations play a vital role in promoting economic development in Somalia. They provide financial support and mentorship to entrepreneurs, helping them establish and grow businesses. By fostering entrepreneurship and economic empowerment, these organizations contribute to poverty reduction and economic stability.

It is essential for diplomats, educators, teachers, journalists, politicians, and legislators to understand the significant impact of diaspora organizations on Somalia's development. By recognizing and supporting these initiatives, they can foster partnerships, provide necessary resources, and advocate for policies that enable diaspora organizations to continue their vital work.

In conclusion, diaspora organizations are a driving force behind Somalia's development initiatives. Their contributions in education, healthcare, infrastructure, and economic empowerment are transforming the country and improving the lives of its people. The support and collaboration of diplomats, educators, teachers, journalists, politicians, and legislators are crucial in further harnessing the potential of diaspora organizations for the betterment of Somalia.

Cultural Preservation and Transnational Connections

In the midst of Somalia's tumultuous history, cultural preservation and transnational connections have played a crucial role in maintaining a sense of identity and resilience among its people. Despite the challenges faced by the country, the Somali people have managed to preserve their rich cultural heritage and establish transnational connections that have brought them together as a community.

One of the key aspects of cultural preservation in Somalia is the preservation of traditional practices, such as storytelling, poetry, and music. These cultural expressions serve as a means of transmitting history, values, and beliefs from one generation to the next. Despite the disruptions caused by political instability and conflict, Somali artists, musicians, and poets have continued to create and perform, ensuring the survival of their cultural traditions.

Additionally, transnational connections have been vital in maintaining the Somali community's unity and resilience. The Somali diaspora, scattered across the globe, has played a significant role in preserving and promoting Somali culture. Through cultural events, language schools, and community organizations, the diaspora has managed to keep Somali traditions alive and pass them on to younger generations.

Moreover, transnational connections have also facilitated the exchange of ideas and resources between Somalia and other nations. Somali students studying abroad have brought back knowledge and skills that can contribute to the country's development. Similarly, international organizations, educators, and policymakers have collaborated with Somali counterparts to support cultural preservation efforts and provide resources for educational initiatives.

However, it is crucial to acknowledge the challenges faced in preserving Somali culture and strengthening transnational connections. Political instability and conflict have often disrupted cultural preservation efforts, leading to the loss of historical artifacts and the displacement of communities. Additionally, limited access to resources and infrastructure has hindered the development of cultural institutions and initiatives.

To address these challenges, it is essential for diplomats, educators, teachers, journalists, politicians, and legislators to recognize the importance of cultural preservation and transnational connections in Somalia. By supporting initiatives that promote cultural expression, such as art exhibitions, literary festivals, and music concerts, they can contribute to the preservation of Somali culture. Additionally, policymakers and educators can collaborate to integrate Somali history, language, and arts into educational curricula, ensuring that future generations have a strong connection to their cultural heritage.

In conclusion, cultural preservation and transnational connections have played a vital role in sustaining the resilience and identity of the Somali people. Despite the challenges faced, the Somali community has managed to preserve their cultural traditions and establish connections that transcend borders. By recognizing the importance of cultural preservation and supporting transnational initiatives, diplomats, educators, teachers, journalists, politicians, and legislators can contribute to the continued resilience and development of Somalia.

Somali Arts, Music, and Literature Abroad

Somalia's rich cultural heritage extends far beyond its borders, with vibrant arts, music, and literature flourishing in Somali diaspora communities around the world. Despite the turmoil and conflict that have plagued Somalia, these creative expressions have persevered, serving as powerful symbols of resilience and identity for Somalis living abroad.

The Somali diaspora has played a vital role in preserving and promoting Somali arts, music, and literature. As diplomats, educators, teachers, journalists, politicians, and legislators, it is important to recognize the significance of these cultural expressions in fostering a sense of unity and belonging among the Somali diaspora community.

One of the most prominent forms of artistic expression is Somali music, which has gained international recognition for its unique blend of traditional Somali melodies with modern influences. Somali musicians abroad have formed bands, organized concerts, and released albums, using their creative talents to connect with their homeland and spread awareness about Somali culture. From London to Minneapolis, Somali music has found a global audience, transcending borders and bringing people together.

Similarly, Somali literature has thrived among the diaspora, with Somali authors penning powerful novels, poetry, and memoirs that capture the essence of the Somali experience. These literary works provide a platform for Somali voices to be heard and understood, shedding light on the struggles, aspirations, and resilience of the Somali people. By showcasing the richness of Somali literature, diplomats, educators, and journalists can contribute to a deeper understanding of Somali culture and history.

In addition to music and literature, Somali visual arts have also flourished in diaspora communities. Somali artists abroad have used various mediums to express their cultural heritage and explore themes of identity, displacement, and resilience. Their artwork often serves as a powerful commentary on the socio-political issues facing Somalia and the diaspora community, creating dialogue and fostering a greater understanding among diverse audiences.

Overall, Somali arts, music, and literature abroad serve as a testament to the enduring spirit of the Somali people. Despite the challenges and pain that Somalia has faced throughout its history, these creative expressions continue to inspire, educate, and unite. As diplomats, educators, teachers, journalists, politicians, and legislators, it is crucial to support and promote Somali arts, music, and literature, recognizing their role in preserving cultural identity, building bridges, and fostering resilience within the Somali diaspora community.

Influence of Diaspora on Somali Identity and Culture

The Somali diaspora has played a significant role in shaping the identity and culture of the Somali people, both within Somalia and in the countries where they have settled. This subchapter explores the various ways in which the diaspora has influenced Somali identity and culture, and the contributions it has made to the development of the Somali community.

One of the key ways in which the diaspora has influenced Somali identity is through the preservation and promotion of Somali language and culture. As Somalis have dispersed around the world, they have worked diligently to maintain their cultural traditions, language, and values. Somali community centers, cultural events, and schools have been established in many countries, providing a platform for cultural exchange and the transmission of Somali heritage to younger generations. This has helped to foster a sense of pride and belonging among Somali people, even in the face of displacement and adversity.

Furthermore, the diaspora has also made significant contributions to the development of Somalia, particularly in the areas of education, healthcare, and entrepreneurship. Many Somali professionals and intellectuals living abroad have returned to Somalia to share their knowledge and expertise, contributing to the rebuilding and development of the country. Additionally, remittances sent by the diaspora to their families in Somalia have provided a crucial lifeline for many people, helping to alleviate poverty and stimulate economic growth.

The influence of the diaspora extends beyond the borders of Somalia. Somali communities in various countries have become important cultural ambassadors, promoting Somali arts, music, and literature. Somali artists, writers, and musicians living abroad have gained international recognition, showcasing the richness and diversity of Somali culture to global audiences. This has not only helped to counter negative stereotypes and misconceptions about Somalia but has also instilled a sense of pride and unity among the Somali diaspora.

In conclusion, the Somali diaspora has had a profound influence on Somali identity and culture. Through their efforts to preserve and promote Somali language and traditions, their contributions to the development of Somalia, and their role as cultural ambassadors, the diaspora has played a vital role in shaping the Somali community both within Somalia and abroad. By recognizing and celebrating the contributions of the diaspora, we can gain a deeper understanding of the resilience and strength of the Somali people and work towards a brighter future for Somalia and its diaspora community.

Chapter 7: Clan Dynamics in Somalia: Influence on Politics and Society

Clan Structures and Traditional Power Dynamics

Introduction:

In the complex landscape of Somalia's political and social fabric, clan structures and traditional power dynamics play a significant role. Understanding the influence of clans on politics and society is crucial for diplomats, educators, journalists, politicians, and legislators seeking to navigate the country's history and contemporary challenges. This subchapter delves into the intricate web of clan dynamics, shedding light on their influence, implications, and interplay with other factors shaping Somalia's trajectory.

Historical Significance of Clans:

Clans have long been the building blocks of Somali society, serving as the bedrock of identity, governance, and conflict resolution. These extended kinship networks have historically provided social cohesion, security, and economic support to their members. However, as Somalia's history has been marred by internal strife, clan identities have also been exploited to fuel divisions and power struggles, leading to political instability and violence.

Clan Influence on Politics:

In Somalia, politics and clan affiliations are deeply intertwined. Clan elders, known as oday, have traditionally held significant authority and were responsible for mediating disputes and making decisions based on consensus. In modern times, this influence has extended to the national level, where clan-based political parties and power-sharing arrangements have emerged. Understanding these dynamics is crucial for diplomats and politicians seeking to engage with Somali leaders and facilitate conflict resolution processes.

Impact on Society:

Clan structures permeate various aspects of Somali society, impacting social relations, economic opportunities, and access to resources. Clan affiliation often determines employment opportunities, access to education, and even marriage prospects. This subchapter explores the implications of these dynamics on social cohesion, equality, and the challenges faced by marginalized groups, including women, youth, and minority clans.

Interplay with Other Factors:

While clan structures undoubtedly shape Somali politics and society, it is essential to examine their interplay with other factors, such as economic disparities, religious identity, and regional rivalries. By acknowledging the complexity and multifaceted nature of these dynamics, diplomats, educators, and journalists can gain a more nuanced understanding of Somalia's challenges and contribute to effective interventions.

Moving Forward:

Recognizing the central role of clan structures and traditional power dynamics in Somalia is crucial for those seeking to promote stability, peace, and development in the country. By engaging with clan leaders, supporting grassroots reconciliation efforts, and promoting inclusive governance, diplomats, educators, and politicians can contribute to building a society where clan identities are harnessed positively and where the aspirations of all Somalis are heard and respected.

Conclusion:

Clan structures and traditional power dynamics continue to shape politics and society in Somalia. Acknowledging their historical significance, understanding their influence on politics and society, and exploring their interplay with other factors is essential for policymakers, educators, and journalists. By delving into this complex web of clan dynamics, we can contribute to a deeper understanding of

Somalia's painful history, its current challenges, and the opportunities for resilience, stability, and development in the future.

Major Somali Clans and Their Roles

The intricate clan dynamics in Somalia have played a significant role in shaping the country's political landscape and societal structure. Understanding the major Somali clans and their roles is essential to comprehending the complexities of Somali society and politics. This subchapter aims to provide an overview of the major Somali clans and their historical significance.

The Somali clans are organized into larger kinship groups known as subclans, which are further divided into lineages and sub-lineages. While it is impossible to cover every single clan in Somalia, some of the most influential clans will be discussed here.

One of the largest and most influential clans is the Darod clan, which is divided into subclans such as the Marehan, Ogaden, and Majerteen. The Darod clan has historically held positions of power, with several Somali presidents hailing from this clan. They have also played a significant role in the Somali Civil War and subsequent political developments.

Another major clan is the Hawiye clan, which includes subclans like the Habar Gidir, Abgaal, and Murursade. The Hawiye clan has been heavily involved in the political landscape of Somalia and has produced prominent political leaders. They have also been influential in the business sector and have a strong presence in Mogadishu.

The Isaaq clan, primarily concentrated in the self-declared independent state of Somaliland, is another significant clan in Somalia. The Isaaq clan has been at the forefront of the political struggle for Somaliland's recognition as an independent state. They have played a vital role in shaping the region's governance and institutions.

The Rahanweyn clan, predominantly inhabiting the southern regions of Somalia, is known for its agricultural expertise. They have traditionally played a vital role in food production and have contributed significantly to the country's economy.

These major clans, along with others such as the Dir, Digil, and Jareer, have shaped Somalia's political landscape, with clan affiliations often determining access to power and resources. Clan dynamics have influenced political alliances, conflicts, and even economic opportunities.

Understanding the roles and influence of these major Somali clans is crucial for diplomats, educators, journalists, and politicians working in Somalia. It allows for a deeper understanding of the country's power dynamics, political struggles, and societal structure. By acknowledging and respecting the influence of clans, stakeholders can work towards a more inclusive and stable Somalia, fostering dialogue and cooperation among the diverse clan groups.

Clan-Based Conflict Resolution Mechanisms

In Somalia, clan-based conflict resolution mechanisms have played a significant role in managing disputes and maintaining social order for centuries. These mechanisms are deeply rooted in the country's traditional clan system, which forms the basis of social and political organization. Understanding these mechanisms is crucial for diplomats, educators, teachers, journalists, politicians, and legislators when engaging with Somalia's complex dynamics.

Clan-based conflict resolution mechanisms are based on the principles of negotiation, mediation, and consensus-building. When conflicts arise, clans appoint respected elders as mediators, known as "Xeer guddoomiyaha," to facilitate dialogue and find resolutions. These elders possess extensive knowledge of customary laws, known as "Xeer," which guide their decision-making processes.

Xeer, a traditional Somali legal system, is based on a code of conduct that emphasizes reconciliation, restitution, and compensation rather than punishment. It provides a framework for resolving disputes, ranging from minor disagreements to more significant conflicts. The elders, through their wisdom and experience, interpret and apply Xeer to find fair and just solutions.

One essential aspect of clan-based conflict resolution mechanisms is the concept of "blood compensation," or "Diya." Diya is a practice where the perpetrator compensates the victim's clan with livestock, money, or other assets as a form of restitution. This practice aims to restore harmony and prevent further escalation of violence.

While clan-based conflict resolution mechanisms have been effective in managing disputes within the Somali society, they face challenges in the modern context. The prolonged civil war and political instability have weakened the traditional structures, resulting in the emergence of alternative mechanisms like Sharia courts and other informal justice systems.

However, efforts have been made to integrate traditional clan-based conflict resolution mechanisms into the formal justice system. In some regions, local courts collaborate with customary elders to ensure that justice is accessible and culturally appropriate. This hybrid approach combines the strengths of both traditional and formal systems and promotes the rule of law while respecting Somali cultural values.

Understanding and supporting clan-based conflict resolution mechanisms is crucial for sustainable peacebuilding efforts in Somalia. External actors should recognize the value of these mechanisms and incorporate them into their engagement strategies. By doing so, they can help strengthen the capacity of local communities to resolve conflicts peacefully, promote social cohesion, and contribute to the overall stability and development of the country.

In conclusion, clan-based conflict resolution mechanisms have long been an integral part of Somalia's social fabric. These mechanisms, rooted in traditional clan systems and guided by customary laws, have played a vital role in managing conflicts and maintaining social order. While facing challenges in the modern context, efforts to integrate these mechanisms into the formal justice system are underway. Recognizing and supporting these mechanisms is crucial for sustainable peacebuilding in Somalia.

Clanism in Politics: Challenges and Opportunities

In the complex political landscape of Somalia, clanism has been a defining feature. The influence of clans on politics and society has shaped the country's history, posing both challenges and opportunities for its people. This subchapter explores the dynamics of clanism in Somali politics and delves into the potential it holds for positive change.

Clanism, or the strong identification with one's clan, has had a significant impact on the political landscape of Somalia. It has often been a source of conflict, as competing clans vie for power and resources. This has led to a history of violence and instability, with clan-based militias and warlords controlling different parts of the country. The Somali Civil War, which erupted in the early 1990s, was a direct consequence of these clan-based divisions and power struggles.

However, amidst the challenges, there are also opportunities for positive change. Clanism can be harnessed as a tool for peacebuilding and reconciliation. Understanding the intricate clan dynamics and engaging with clan leaders can help in resolving conflicts and fostering stability. By involving clans in the political process, their grievances can be addressed, and their influence can be channeled towards constructive ends.

Moreover, clanism can be transformed into a force for social cohesion and development. The strong sense of identity and loyalty that clans evoke can be utilized to build strong institutions and foster a sense of collective responsibility. By integrating clan dynamics into governance structures, it is possible to create inclusive policies that accommodate the diverse interests and needs of different clans. This can help in fostering a sense of belonging and ownership among the Somali people and pave the way for sustainable development.

However, it is crucial to strike a balance between clan-based politics and the need for a unified national identity. While clanism can be a source of strength, it can also be a source of division if it is allowed to dominate the political arena. Therefore, efforts should be made to promote a sense of Somali nationalism that transcends clan affiliations. This can be achieved through the promotion of shared values, history, and aspirations that unite all Somalis.

In conclusion, clanism in Somali politics poses both challenges and opportunities. While it has been a source of conflict and instability, it also holds the potential for peacebuilding, reconciliation, and social cohesion. By understanding and engaging with clan dynamics, Somalia can harness the positive aspects of clanism and transform it into a force for development and progress.

Electoral Politics and Clan Representation

In the complex political landscape of Somalia, the role of electoral politics and clan representation cannot be underestimated. Somalia has a history of clan-based politics, where clans have played a significant role in shaping political alliances and power structures. This subchapter aims to delve into the dynamics of electoral politics and clan representation in Somalia, exploring their impact on society and governance.

Electoral politics in Somalia has been marked by a delicate balance between clan representation and the need for broader national unity. Clan affiliations have traditionally played a crucial role in determining political representation and electoral outcomes. This can be attributed to the deep-rooted clan-based social structure and the historical significance of kinship ties in Somali society.

However, the overreliance on clan representation has often led to challenges in achieving an inclusive and representative political system. Clan affiliations have at times overshadowed meritocracy and hindered the formation of broad-based political parties. This has resulted in a political landscape fragmented along clan lines, making it difficult to build a cohesive and stable government.

Despite these challenges, efforts have been made to promote more inclusive electoral processes. The 2012 and 2016 parliamentary elections in Somalia, for instance, marked a shift towards a more representative system. These elections aimed to strike a balance between clan representation and the need for a more merit-based approach. While clan elders still played a role in the selection of candidates, efforts were made to ensure a broader participation of the population in the voting process.

The influence of clan dynamics on electoral politics extends beyond the election process itself. Clan affiliations often shape political alliances and power-sharing agreements among different factions. This has both positive and negative implications for governance and stability. On one hand, clan-based alliances can foster consensus-building and promote inclusivity. On the other hand, they can also perpetuate divisions and rivalries that impede effective governance.

To address these challenges, there is a need for continued efforts to promote a more inclusive and representative political system in Somalia. This includes supporting the development of strong political parties that transcend clan boundaries and encouraging the participation of marginalized groups, such as women and minorities, in the political process. Furthermore, efforts should be made to strengthen democratic institutions and promote transparency and accountability in the electoral process.

In conclusion, electoral politics and clan representation are intertwined in the complex political landscape of Somalia. While clan affiliations have historically played a significant role in shaping political alliances and representation, the overreliance on clan dynamics has presented challenges to achieving an inclusive and representative political system. Efforts should be made to strike a balance between clan representation and broader national unity, promoting the development of strong political parties and inclusive electoral processes. By doing so, Somalia can pave the way for a more stable and prosperous future.

Clan Alliances and Political Fragmentation

In the turbulent history of Somalia, clan alliances and political fragmentation have played a pivotal role in shaping the country's political landscape. Understanding the complex dynamics of clan affiliations and their impact on governance is essential for diplomats, educators, teachers, journalists, politicians, and legislators who seek to grasp the intricacies of Somalia's political situation.

Somalia's clan system is deeply rooted in the social fabric of the country, with clans serving as the primary unit of identity and loyalty. These clans are extended kinship groups that provide a sense of belonging and security to their members. However, the importance of clans extends beyond cultural and social ties, as they also influence political power and decision-making processes.

Historically, clan alliances have been both a source of strength and a cause of political fragmentation in Somalia. Various clans have formed alliances to consolidate power and gain influence over the central government. These alliances have often resulted in power struggles and conflicts, as different clans compete for resources, representation, and control.

Political fragmentation has been a recurring theme in Somalia's history, with the central government struggling to assert its authority over the various regions and clans. This fragmentation has hindered the establishment of a stable and unified government, leading to prolonged periods of political instability and violence.

The impact of clan alliances and political fragmentation on Somalia's society and governance cannot be overstated. Clan-based politics have often overshadowed meritocracy and hindered the development of inclusive and accountable governance structures. This has perpetuated a cycle of corruption, nepotism, and conflict, undermining efforts to establish a functioning state.

Addressing the challenges posed by clan alliances and political fragmentation requires a comprehensive understanding of Somalia's history, culture, and social dynamics. It necessitates a nuanced approach that balances the recognition of clan identities with the promotion of inclusive and democratic governance.

Efforts to mitigate the negative effects of clan-based politics should focus on promoting dialogue and reconciliation among different clans, fostering trust-building initiatives, and strengthening institutions that are inclusive and accountable. A multi-stakeholder approach involving diplomats, educators, teachers, journalists, politicians, and legislators is crucial in supporting Somalia's journey towards stability, peace, and sustainable development.

By engaging with the complexities of clan alliances and political fragmentation, the international community can contribute to Somalia's progress and resilience. It is through a deep understanding of these dynamics that effective policies and interventions can be formulated to address the challenges faced by the Somali people and pave the way for a brighter future.

Moving Beyond Clan Politics: National Unity and Reconciliation

In a country ravaged by decades of conflict and political instability, one of the biggest challenges facing Somalia today is moving beyond clan politics and towards national unity and reconciliation. This subchapter explores the importance of overcoming divisions based on clan affiliations, and the potential for a unified Somalia that embraces diversity and inclusivity.

Clan dynamics have long played a significant role in Somali politics and society. The deep-rooted clan system, with its intricate network of alliances and rivalries, has shaped the country's history and contributed to its ongoing struggles. However, it is crucial to recognize that clan politics alone cannot build a stable and prosperous nation. The path to a peaceful Somalia lies in promoting national unity and reconciliation, transcending the barriers of clan divisions.

National unity is essential for a country to thrive and overcome the challenges it faces. It requires a collective effort from all segments of society, including diplomats, educators, teachers, journalists, politicians, and legislators. These stakeholders have a crucial role to play in fostering a sense of shared identity and purpose among Somalis, emphasizing the idea of a united Somalia rather than one divided by clan lines.

Reconciliation is another vital component in the journey towards national unity. The wounds of the past must be healed, and grievances addressed in a fair and transparent manner. This requires a comprehensive truth and reconciliation process, where all parties involved can come together to acknowledge past wrongs, seek forgiveness, and chart a new path forward. International support and expertise will be invaluable in facilitating this process.

The subchapter also highlights the importance of education and cultural expression in promoting national unity. Educators and teachers have a responsibility to teach future generations about the shared history and values of Somalia, emphasizing the importance of unity and tolerance. Artists, writers, and cultural figures can contribute by using their platforms to promote dialogue, understanding, and reconciliation.

Ultimately, moving beyond clan politics and towards national unity and reconciliation is not an easy task. It requires the commitment and collaboration of all stakeholders involved, as well as a long-term vision for a united and prosperous Somalia. By embracing diversity, addressing past grievances, and promoting a sense of shared identity, Somalia can overcome its painful history and build a brighter future for its people.

Efforts to Depoliticize Clans and Promote National Identity

In the tumultuous history of Somalia, clans have played a central role in shaping the political landscape and social fabric of the country. However, their influence has often hindered the establishment of a strong national identity and has been a source of political instability. Recognizing the need to depoliticize clans and promote a sense of national unity, various efforts have been made to address this issue.

One of the key strategies employed to depoliticize clans and foster a national identity is the promotion of inclusive governance structures. By ensuring equal representation and participation of all clans in decision-making processes, it becomes possible to dilute the influence of individual clans and create a more inclusive political system. This has been achieved through the establishment of representative bodies, such as the Transitional Federal Government and subsequent federal governments, which aim to bring together representatives from different clans to work towards a common goal.

Education has also been identified as a crucial tool in promoting national identity. By incorporating a comprehensive curriculum that emphasizes the shared history, values, and traditions of all Somalis, schools can play a vital role in shaping the collective consciousness of the younger generation. Efforts have been made to revise the curriculum to include a more balanced representation of the diverse Somali population and to promote national unity.

Media and communication channels have been effectively utilized to promote national identity and depoliticize clans. Through radio, television, and online platforms, messages of unity, tolerance, and shared aspirations are disseminated to the wider population. This helps to counter divisive narratives and foster a sense of belonging to a larger Somali nation.

International organizations and foreign governments have also played a significant role in supporting efforts to depoliticize clans and promote national identity. Diplomatic engagement, capacity-building initiatives, and financial support have been extended to Somalia to strengthen national institutions, encourage peaceful dialogue, and promote reconciliation among different clans.

While progress has been made, challenges remain in depoliticizing clans and promoting national identity in Somalia. Clan dynamics continue to exert influence on politics and society, and the process of building a strong national identity is an ongoing endeavor. However, through sustained efforts and a commitment to inclusive governance, education, media, and international cooperation, Somalia can gradually move towards a more unified and politically stable future.

Role of Civil Society in

Role of Civil Society in Somalia: Building a Path to Stability and Development

Introduction:

In the turbulent history of Somalia, the role of civil society has been crucial in fostering stability, promoting development, and addressing the challenges faced by the nation. This subchapter explores the significant contributions of civil society actors in Somalia and their impact on various aspects of society. From advocating for peace to promoting gender equality, civil society organizations have played a pivotal role in shaping the nation's trajectory.

Importance of Civil Society:

Civil society, comprising non-governmental organizations (NGOs), community-based organizations, and grassroots movements, has emerged as a vital force in Somalia. In the absence of a strong central government, civil society has filled the governance gap, providing essential services, advocating for human rights, and promoting social cohesion.

Promoting Peace and Reconciliation:

One of the primary roles of civil society in Somalia has been to facilitate peace and reconciliation efforts. Through dialogue, mediation, and community engagement, civil society organizations have played a key role in resolving conflicts at the local level and fostering national reconciliation. Their efforts have been instrumental in rebuilding trust, promoting social cohesion, and preventing the recurrence of violence.

Advocating for Human Rights and Gender Equality:

Civil society groups in Somalia have been at the forefront of advocating for human rights and gender equality. They have worked tirelessly to address the marginalization and discrimination faced by vulnerable groups, including women, minorities, and refugees. By raising awareness, lobbying for policy changes, and providing support services, civil society organizations have contributed significantly to advancing human rights and fostering inclusive development.

Providing Essential Services:

In a country devastated by decades of conflict, civil society organizations have stepped in to provide essential services in areas such as healthcare, education, and livelihood support. Their presence and commitment have been critical in addressing the needs of communities, particularly in remote and conflict-affected regions where government services are scarce.

Enhancing Development and Governance:

Civil society actors have also played a crucial role in promoting good governance, transparency, and accountability in Somalia. By monitoring government actions, advocating for policy reforms, and engaging in grassroots mobilization, civil society organizations have contributed to building a more accountable and inclusive state.

Conclusion:

The role of civil society in Somalia cannot be understated. From promoting peace and reconciliation to advocating for human rights and providing essential services, civil society organizations have been pivotal in shaping the nation's trajectory. In a country struggling with political instability, conflict, and economic challenges, their contributions are vital in building a path towards stability, resilience, and sustainable development. As diplomats, educators, journalists, and policymakers, it is imperative to recognize and support the critical role of civil society in Somalia's journey towards a brighter future. By working collaboratively with civil society actors, we can help foster a more inclusive, peaceful, and prosperous Somalia for all its citizens.

www.ingramcontent.com/pod-product-compliance
Lightning Source LLC
Chambersburg PA
CBHW031432150726
47989CB00002B/908